The Modern Girl's Guide to Life

Sarah-Kate Lynch

RANDOM HOUSE
NEW ZEALAND

For bosoms past, present and future.

A RANDOM HOUSE BOOK
published by
Random House New Zealand
18 Poland Road, Glenfield, Auckland, New Zealand
www.randomhouse.co.nz

First published 2002
© 2002 Sarah-Kate Lynch
The moral rights of the author have been asserted
ISBN 1 86941 55 66

Design: Elin Termannsen
Cover and inside illustrations: Holly Roach
Cover design: Thoughtfields
Printed: Publishing Press

Contents

Nibbles and Tipples
- Cocktails — 10
- Smorgasbords — 12
- Barbecues — 14
- Wine — 16
- Blowing in the Bag — 18
- Guilt — 20

Glad Rags and Sad Rags
- Jeans — 24
- Knickers — 26
- That Special Outfit — 28
- Pashminas — 30
- Colour — 32
- Internet Shopping — 34
- Windbreakers — 36

Our Four-Legged Friends
- Pet-sitting — 40
- Pooches — 42

Every Home Should Have One
- Gingers — 46
- Baldness — 48
- Valentines — 50
- Slavery — 52
- Camping — 54
- House-sitting — 56

The Crappy Wanderer
- Moving — 60
- The Road Trip — 62
- Moving Again — 64

Elbows, Knees and Whoops-a-daisy

Behinds	68
Hair Removal	70
The Fat Farm	72
Tanning	74
Hair	76
PMT	78
Summer	80
Legs	82
Diets	84

Good On Ya, Sport

Exercise	88
Skiing	90
Fishing	92
Olympics	94
Tramping	96
The Routeburn Track	98

Wrinkles and Rankles

Ageing	102
Facials	104
Parties	106
Bars	108
Spots	110
Undergarments	112

In the House

Reality TV	116
Computers	118
Tradesmen	120
Domestic Bliss	122

The Big Wide World

Irish Roots	126
More Irish Roots	128
The City of Angels	130
The Big Apple	132

Paris	134
Irish Weather	136
Nails	138

Modern Girls

Girly Weekends	142
Baby Waxing	144
Swearing	146
The Economy	148
Book Clubs	150
Changing Rooms	152
The Sound of Music	154
Columnists	156
Personalised Plates	158
Baches	160
Knitting	162
Sleep	164
Sisters	166

Doing It Yourself

Rectangles	170
Painting	172
Living with Mum	174
Hard Yakka	176

The Festive Season

That Time of Year	180
Drinks	182
Christmas	184
The Christmas After	186
New Year	188
Another New Year	190

From the Author

Who ever thought I would write enough columns to pick out a selection and put them in a book? It gives me a warm feeling in my tummy just thinking about it – unless that's the steak and kidney pie I had for pre-morning tea making itself comfortable down below.

Anyway, it's been three and a half years since I kidnapped the editor of the *New Zealand Woman's Weekly* and tortured her until she let me have my own column and now that her bruises have finally faded, she even lets me come to the office sometimes. On Sundays. After 11pm.

Now, here I am with Volume I of "The Collection" as I now know it.

You may be interested to know that looking over the 200-odd columns (or should that be 200 odd columns) to select the juiciest made me realise two things. One: even a boring life like mine can be jazzed up with a few well-placed fibs. Two: I really have to get over paying $200 for my pashmina.

People ask me if I have trouble coming up with ideas week after week and I can happily report that no, I don't. The good thing about writing a column poking fun at turgid old everyday life is that turgid old everyday life is right there being lived by you and, ripe for the plucking.

At one point, early on in the column-writing, I think there was some suggestion that I concentrated on food too much: eating it and the after-effects on my thighs.

I tried, then, to eliminate all talk of comestibles and other ingestibles and avoid all talk of body parts and the clothes that never fit them.

Sadly, this left me with nothing to say. The truth is that like many modern girls my preoccupation with eating and dieting and shopping and exercising takes up quite a lot of my day and what's left I devote to taunting my poor beleaguered husband over the size of his brain. Why, it's barely bigger than a pea and nowhere near such a nice colour.

So, rocket science *The Modern Girl's Guide to Life* ain't.

But hopefully it might brighten up a day otherwise dulled by large vats of washing, small snot-nosed children, bunions, too much chocolate, not enough chocolate or PMT.

The columns have been grouped together in clumps of similar subjects, rather than in chronological order. In fact, I seem never to be in the same place for more than approximately five minutes which isn't really the case although I got a right old shock upon reading "New Year" (page 188).

It starts off with me resolving to "never, ever, as long as I live, as long as there's life in these bones and breath in these lungs, not for all the tea in China – or India, where it mostly comes from these days – am I ever, ever, EVER going to move again. Ever."

This was written for New Year 2000/2001 and I am aghast to report that I have moved twice since then. From one end of the country to the other and back again. Obviously my request that someone track me down and give me a good slapping should I start picking up empty cardboard boxes again fell on deaf ears.

I must never, ever as long as I live etc. say I will never, ever do anything ever again.

But then that's real life, isn't it. We don't always do what we say we are going to and quite often do what we said we wouldn't. We spend years promising to start our diets tomorrow. We keep the jeans we fitted into 23 years ago but now can't get past our ankles. We join the gym and go once, yet renew our membership. We love our dogs/cats/handbags more than our husbands. We spend money on creams that we know can't possibly make our wrinkles go away (unless it's Polyfilla) and we dream of having sex with Brad Pitt even though we really like Jennifer Aniston and anyway, we wouldn't want him to see us with no clothes on.

We're modern girls. And these are the trials of our everyday life.

Sarah-Kate

Nibbles and Tipples

Cocktails

AS I'M ABOUT TO JET OFF to the islands for the sacred and holy nuptials of some dearly beloved friends, my mind has naturally turned to cocktails.

There can't be too many experiences in the whole wild world more pleasant than lying under a shady tree on a sparkling, sunny day, a Jackie Collins novel open and panting on one side of you and a fru-fru cocktail with many bits of pineapple and a load of umbrellas on the other.

All the better if you haven't had to pay resort hotel prices, I tell the ginger husband, by way of explaining why I am packing the blender. And the ice trays. And the little umbrellas. And the curly straws. Well, we wouldn't want to run out of money and have to forgo the smorgasbord, I add.

A nano-second's horrified silence is followed by the sound of ginger fingers searching the drawers for the tropical coaster collection. No reason to let standards slip just because we're in foreign parts, he adds, throwing the swizzle sticks in the bag.

Not all cocktails are good, though. In fact, over the years, I have deduced everyone in the world (okay, make that my world) has one cocktail they will never drink again.

In fact, you even have to say the name of this cocktail very quietly, in case the sound of it has a violent effect on the stomach of the tender soul opposed to it.

My friend Sonya feels this way about tequila sunrises. Twenty years ago, she had such a violent reaction to drinking about 47 of them she still, to this day, cannot drink orange juice — never mind the tequila and whatever the red bits are.

Myself, I don't care much for martinis, not after drinking three of them and then spending two hours in the WC of people I had only just met, feeling considerably shaken and stirred. Amazingly, I still know them, just not well enough to ask if they could please burn the picture which was hanging on that bathroom wall 15 years ago, because they still have it and it still makes me want to hurl. (I thought it was a turtle but apparently it's a map of somewhere.)

I've heard quite a few tales of gin making people cry but, frankly, I think that's a good thing. Me, I use Hallmark TV ads and Kosovar refugees but they don't do much for your thirst, or go particularly well with tonic.

A few years after the unfortunate martini experiment, I discovered Brain Erasers. They obviously worked because I can't remember what was in them, except they came in a pint glass and looked milky.

"I'll have two Rain Abrasers," I demanded slurringly of a grouchy barman one night. "Can't say it — can't have it," came the reply. At the time it seemed unforgivably churlish but I have to say, with the wisdom of hindsight, it's not a bad system.

Daiquiris — now I've not heard a bad word said about them. Not a bad word I could understand, that is. Mind you, it's not always easy to make yourself heard when you've a lampshade on your head and someone else's knickers stuffed in your mouth.

Still — a little bit of white rum, a little taste of citrus liqueur, fresh fruit and ice — well, it's practically medicinal, isn't it?

And *so* easy to enunciate.

Smorgasbords

THEY SAY EVERYONE is naturally good at one thing — it's with some relief I've finally found out what my thing is. For a while I thought it was doing the laundry but then the Ginger confessed he'd been doing extra loads behind my back to keep his smalls coming through on time.

Then I tried cooking, which wasn't a total disaster but it turns out I'm good at drinking the cooking wine and not good at cleaning up the kitchen, which somehow cancels everything out.

You can imagine my delight, then, to discover, on my sojourn to a Fijian island resort, where my real skill lies — smorgasbording. Looking back, I think my nearest and dearest may have suspected this and attempted to repress my natural talent by veering me away from this style of dining. Leastways, they've often looked scared when I've mentioned the buffet as an eating option.

Put me on a tiny island with only the smorgasbord for sustenance, though, and there is no keeping my light under a bushel (even if it's the biggest bushel in Christendom).

It was shock which first brought out my natural all-you-can-eat aptitude. I had been asked to jump on the scales at the mainland airport before being allowed to embark on the final leg of my journey to the island resort. Despite my protestations that I'd written an entire book about avoiding the bathroom scales, despite the hi-jacking threats, insulting the pilot and the bribes, a team of 30 strong men emerged out of nowhere and lifted me on to the weighing machine.

A stunned silence swept the busy airport, followed by a low under-the-breath whistle. I was grateful the digital display on my side of the counter was keeping all waiting holiday-makers fully aware of the situation, because it would have been terrible for anyone to miss out.

I was saved somewhat by my backpack, which I was allowed to continue wearing for the weigh-in.

"I've got a ghetto-blaster in here," I explained to the crowd forming around the scales. "I have the blender I bought in the KMart sale. I have enough alcohol to make approximately 1000 daiquiris. I have an iron. I have bricks in case any foundations prove to be shaky. I have bars of lead."

But the rabble was losing interest and moving away.

"I have gluten-free loaves of bread," I yelled after them, but by this stage the 30 strong men were carrying me out to insert me into the plane.

"I didn't mean what I said about your mother," I told the pilot. Boy, whoever thought there could be so much turbulence on a still, sunny day?

No wonder I needed to settle my stomach upon arrival at my destination. And there, like an oasis in the middle of a tropical island, lay the smorgasbord.

Like a panther I moved through the queues of thin people and started loading up my plate. Beetroot, corn, cold meat, sausages, potatoes, rolls, lettuce (not too much), slices of plastic cheese, six different sauces, pineapple, shrimps, sponge cake, chicken drumsticks, fries from the kids' corner, another six sauces, jelly, something small and round I couldn't identify and lasagne.

Staggering under the weight of my expertly stacked plate, the horror of the weigh-in now behind me, I suddenly felt good about myself. It's definitely my thing.

Barbecues

YOU WOULD THINK that, by now, the sight of one more sausage sizzling on a barbecue plate would be enough to turn you on to vegetarian patties forever. But it seems, in my case anyway, there is no such thing as too much meat grilled alfresco. Who knew? My arteries must be hardening as I speak.

This summer, we're eating even more meat than usual as the Ginger recently purchased a new barbecue with a small windfall from lotto (another 156 wins and we'll be even). The buying process seemed to take quite a long time and I can only thank God that there is no publication named *BBQ Trader* or I wouldn't have got a word of sense out of him for months.

In the end, he went for one with stainless steel bits and a fancy cover. The stainless steel never rusts, he told me. Lasts a lifetime.

"So why the fancy cover?" I asked. "Should we not have bought a fancy cover for our last barbecue," I wondered, "which wasn't made of stainless steel, rusted and therefore ended its lifetime at the tip?"

What followed was a long line of technical reasons which, frankly, didn't add up to much but I couldn't really argue. He was buying a meal-making device after all.

He considers the barbecue his domain and I'd be a fool to mess with that. Why, it'll be the depths of winter before he realises he's been cooking three meals a day on that contraption while I've been sitting serenely on the sofa, flicking through TV channels and talking on the phone.

The salads, according to some unwritten rule, become the responsibility of the person who doesn't do the barbecuing but I've never showed much skill in this department. To me, a salad is just lettuce, cucumber and tomato with a boiled egg if you're lucky and lashings of mayonnaise.

And I don't mean your fancy rocket, cos or mesclun (whatever that is and however you spell it, although I'm sure it's not "mesculin") lettuce either. I mean good old-fashioned iceberg.

As far as I am concerned, the purpose of the salad is to lie prettily at the side of the meat goods, providing some colour and a notion of health. It's like the gym. It's the joining that counts. You don't actually have to go. So with salads, eating them is not essential.

The Ginger (not to mention VegFed) doesn't entirely agree with me on this, which is to say he doesn't eat *my* salads but wolfs them down with alacrity if someone else makes them.

In a bid to spice up his greens recently, while not breaking the rules and still devoting most of my evenings to channel surfing, I came up with the exciting new concept of barbecued salads. Floppy courgettes, pepper remains, manky mushrooms — whatever lies at the bottom of the fridge you will now find out there sizzling up a storm alongside the steaks and snarlers. I've even managed to get good old Ginge to barbecue potatoes.

Actually, I've got so much spare time on my hands when it comes time to cook dinner these days that I may have to get digital TV. I need the extra channels.

Wine

I LIKE A TIPPLE, ME. Have I mentioned that in the past? Goodness but my memory isn't what it used to be.

Where was I? Oh yes, wine is my snifter of choice and, when it comes to what I like and what I don't, I am exceptionally knowledgeable and excruciatingly choosy.

Well, it has to be white.

Or red if the white's run out.

My interest in wine first developed when, as the tallest of my teenage friends, I was usually the first to be dispatched to the liquor store for a bottle of their finest Marque Vue.

This was a crime. Nobody should ever have been able to buy Marque Vue or, in fact, any wine which costs less than three bucks a bottle.

Fortunately my taste came over all sophisticated when my late father took to buying wine in large quantities and hiding it — badly — in the garage, whereupon I helped myself whenever the fancy took me.

Unfortunately, after years of paying less than three bucks a bottle, it wasn't my palate which told me my taste had come over all sophisticated, it was the host of a dinner party to which I took a freshly purloined offering.

"Aaaaargh," she cried, snatching it out of my hands. "I just saw this at the fancy wine shop for $28. Thanks!"

Twenty-eight dollars? In 1983? For ONE bottle of wine? Oh, my giddy aunt.

Had I known the stolen stuff was so precious, I would not have pinched it, or at least bothered to read the label and show off a bit before quaffing it. My father, upon eventually finding himself several bottles down, was most unimpressed but, as the discovery was made on my brother's birthday and I cleverly thought to blame the theft on him, the fall-out was minimal — for me anyway.

When I heard wine was only a dollar a litre in Australia I

moved there but even that lure could not make up for the fact far too many conversations revolved around whether six was pronounced sux or sex so, after a couple of years, I went to London.

There, I developed an abiding interest in the Bulgarian varietals of the time, which generally came in under the two-pound mark.

Despite this, the owner of the off-licence across the road still managed a trip back to Bombay on the profit made from our flat alone. Seriously.

By the time I got back to New Zealand, casks were old hat and boutique bottled stuff was all the rage.

Then, just when I got the hang of paying more than a tenner a bottle, some mature adult started sneaking in the concept of food and wine matching and now I'm back in the amateur league.

A lump of cheese on a toothpick I can grasp, but whole meals — how's that going to work?

"I thought you told me eatin' was cheatin'," the Ginger pointed out as I showed him how to combine a buttery chardonnay with, er, something else buttery — some butter in fact.

"It has a hint of asparagus, a suggestion of tinned peas," I sniffed, ignoring him.

"So it will most likely go quite well with the buttery asparagus and tinned pea pie we're eating then?"

Really I don't know why I bother. Training monkeys would have to be more rewarding.

Where was I? Oh yes, I like a tipple, me.

Have I mentioned that in the past?

Blowing in the Bag

I MUST HAVE TAKEN ON the look of a tippler in my old age because the breathalysing brigade just can't get enough of me.

Luckily for me, I don't actually tipple as much as I would appear to. There's a very good reason for that — and not just plain old moderation.

Despite my love of a glass or two of giggle juice, I live 40 minutes out of town and only two buses go there (one on a Tuesday and one on a Friday), so I rely heavily on my motor. Should it be taken away from me in an awful over-tippling incident, it would spell disaster. And a lot of hitch-hiking.

Plus, I'm still so scared of my third-form teacher, Sister Eulalia, that, should I do wrong, never mind what the legal system would do to me, the thought of Sister Eulalia rising from the grave for a tongue-lashing helps keep me on the straight and narrow.

Yes, in short, I am not a bloody idiot.

Last month, though, I was stopped by the police at midday, out in the middle of nowhere, for the purposes of breathalysation. While I had not been into the cooking sherry, I was driving an unfamiliar car and being stopped by the police for some reason rendered me incapable of finding the button which opened my window, opening the other three by mistake. What is it about men with truncheons that makes one so nervous?

Anyway, just this week I showed remarkable restraint in a free drinks situation. I don't know about you, but it seems much easier to resist a snifter you might have to pay for than one of the complimentary variety.

Two hours, two tipples and large amounts of finger food later, I was once again pulled over by the rozzers and required to blow in the bag.

"You're under the limit. Drive safely and have a good evening," the copper told me, as the dog growled in a sinister fashion from the back seat. (Well, all the back windows were open — why wouldn't he?)

What a contrast to a similar experience earlier in the year, when I was driving home from an important assignment involving a six-course meal and two America's Cup sailors.

Again I was pulled over and blew in the bag, happy in the knowledge my two-glass imbibing was of a responsible nature, given that I'd consumed my own weight in comestibles.

The police boy on the other end of the blower flashed the results in my face and then peered in at me.

"No offence," he started, as he gave me the once-over a second time. "Yes, no offence, but you big, solid people metabolise alcohol much faster than skinny people. If you were 20, I would be taking you to the police station."

What he was trying to tell me was, I was under the limit and should drive safely and have a good evening.

"When it's a crime to be fat and old, you can cuff me," I wanted to tell him. "Until then, I'll be on my way, you pimply pipsqueak."

But the spirit of Sister Eulalia must have been lurking close by, because instead I smiled and thanked the lovely policeman, then took my enormous, aged self home, metabolising as I went.

Guilt

I'M STARTING TO WORRY about what I should be doing with the enormous supply of guilt I seem to be stockpiling.

"There's great lumps of it around the back," the Ginger reported gloomily the other day, overlooking the fact it's really his fault I have such a build-up in the first place.

You see, if I wasn't leading such a, more or less, exemplary married lifestyle I'd have more use for all the guilt which was so delicately crafted over years of convent schooling.

As it is, I'm just a lapsed old goody-two-shoes with very little to repent.

Oh, for the days when one would sob into the hooters of one's Malibu Barbie, aching with remorse at having told whoppers in the confession box owing to not having committed any decent sins.

That's the bona fide sort of bowel-gripping guilt I miss out on these days.

"Perhaps I should commit something totally heinous and get rid of it all at once?" I suggested to the Ginger. "You know, like murder."

"Yes, well," he answered nervously, carefully extracting the carving knife from my hand. "It would certainly keep you from wasting it on whether you gave the boy at the gas station the right sort of smile or not."

"But the wrong sort of smile could ruin a person's day," I cried.

But four hours of hearing me bang on about it could ruin his, he replied. In fact, it definitely had.

Actually, he had a point. The more I thought about it the more I realised I have been frittering my guilt on things which were hardly worthy of it.

Skipping a track on a CD, for example.

I usually apportion a good few units of guilt to this, although, if I'm honest, I know the song I'm missing probably doesn't really mind.

Leaving the dog at home, there's another guilt-waster.

"You absolutely should not feel bad about him," the Ginger railed in an exasperated fashion recently. "He has a brain the size of a walnut. He eats rocks. He doesn't know the difference between a minute and a week. He drinks water out of the toilet."

Yes, well, easy for him to say when it's my back the poor little four-legged creature's eyes bore into as he taps out, "WHATEVER YOU DO, DON'T LEAVE ME," in Morse code with his paws.

At least I think that's what he's saying. It could be his foot just goes bananas when he licks himself in a certain fashion.

Anyway, regardless of the dog's dexterity, there's no doubt I am wasting my guilt and need to find something better to do with it before it can't be tucked neatly away any more and starts bursting out at inappropriate moments.

"You are going to LOVE this," the Ginger said the other night when he burst in the door, a plastic shopping bag in hand.

"Should I love something which might not be biodegradable?" I worried.

"Biodegradable be damned," the Ginger cried, revealing the contents of the plastic bag with a Shakespearian flourish.

Oh, joy. An ice-cream. An ice-cream of half vanilla, half chocolate persuasion. An ice-cream covered in chocolate. Covered again in a deliciously sticky brown goo. Then covered once more with chocolate.

A tonne or two more of these babies and my guilt stocks should be well and truly depleted. Then I'll have nothing to worry about at all.

Glad Rags and Sad Rags

Jeans

ONCE EVERY THREE or four years, I take leave of my senses and go shopping for the perfect pair of jeans.

This expedition always starts in the same way. I leave home, happy in the knowledge I've been skipping the golden arches and other fatty food emporiums for at least a week and am ripe and ready for a splendid new pair of figure-hugging denims.

It always ends the same way, too. I arrive home battered, bruised, sweaty and heaving, crying inconsolably and crawling on all fours towards the cocktail cabinet. Large amounts of potato crisps are the only thing which will bring me around again.

In fact, now I come to think about it, it must be my deep devotion to the potato crisp which gets me back out on the streets for this tri-annual mortification ritual — why else would I do it?

So, subconsciously desirous of a crisp-fest and buoyed by a picture of Roseanne in funky denims, I recently set off to find my next perfect pair of strides.

Shop number one had nothing in my size. Shop number two didn't let me in. Shop number three had heard I was on my way and mysteriously relocated to a secret destination.

I snuck up on shop number four, but, by then, I admit I was a little tense.

I perused the racks of jeans, rigid with the fear one of the stick figures in attendance would ask if I needed help.

Nobody wants to mention their waist measurement out loud, even if they have gone to the trouble of memorising it in centimetres in the hope no one will know what it means.

Going for the Gwyneth look, I plucked a couple of pairs of hipsters and some straight-legged jobs from the shelves and shuffled discreetly into the changing room.

The hipsters were a mistake. Having spent my entire life mocking people with builders' butt-crack, I didn't really feel like displaying one of my own, especially as I didn't think it was supposed to be a feature of those particular jeans. Nor did my midriff (more of a maxriff, really) want baring.

The straight-legged jeans looked great from the knee down but, as usual, one of the little toothpicks started banging on the door, asking how I was getting on, just as I was realising with horror and shame there was a fleshy 10cm gap between the top button and its corresponding hole.

Now, I didn't want to see that myself, let alone frighten some poor defenceless sales assistant with it.

"Um, they're a bit too short," I squeaked, trying desperately to peel myself out of the wretched things. "Do you have anything longer?"

Forty-seven pairs of wide-legged, short-waisted, baggy-fitting, extra-long, 501, 2, 3 and 4s later, everyone in the shop was crying.

"They really do nothing for you, dear," the mother of the girl in the next cubicle whispered tearfully. "Nothing."

Rubbed raw around the waist from fitting mishaps and my fingers bleeding from wretchedly clawing at zippers, I apologised to the hysterical shop assistants, one of whom had been kind enough to rush out and buy a "With Sympathy" card for me, and left, empty-handed.

Lying in the bath with a litre of gin and tonic some hours later, I finally had to admit to myself that ready-salted really is better than salt and vinegar.

Knickers

I KNOW I'VE WRITTEN about knickers before but the thing is I've completely changed my tune. Last time I crowed about finding a comfortable style of stout undergarment that neither rode up one's nether regions nor cut them in two. I purchased an entire set of said pants and proceeded to wear them for a year or three.

But comes a time in a girl's as-late-as-you-can-get thirties when she realises she is too scared to hang her undies on the line in case the local possums see them and take fright, heading away from the bright lights of the nearest road and towards the hills in such numbers that it's possible they could cause an avalanche.

I had one such incident the other day. I realised that my nana pants were hanging where the neighbours could see them. Not only that — they were blocking out the sun over the whole of Central Otago and a cold front was forming near the crotch. In a bid to stop the pending tsunami caused by this dangerous weather pattern, I attempted to move the knickers back a row, where just myself and the dog could see them and the sun still shone.

In the unpegging and re-pegging process however, I managed to lose hold of a pair and I swear as they fell to the ground they caught a gust of wind and inflated to such proportions I was amazed to find there wasn't a German backpacker attached to them. They sailed paratrooper-style earthward and lay enormously in a splodge on the ground.

True, their elastic wasn't what it once was. I may have been excited at finding my sensible knickers but I had not been so excited that I had replaced them in recent times.

On my next visit to Ballantynes department store in Christchurch then, I headed straight for the lingerie department, eschewing anything more than a foot in length or less than five dollars in price.

Half an hour later I emerged with a very hip and funky pair of

Calvin Klein women's boxer shorts and two pairs of Bendon briefs. I spent half of the next day picking the former out of you-know-where but the briefs, well, success seems too small a word.

Two decorative yet substantial stretches of lace at the front gave this knicker a feminine touch that the paratrooper pants had not managed. Looking more high cut on the leg than they actually were, these undies could hold their heads up high on the clothesline, yet not encourage unsightly bulges when worn. And at the rear, well, a girl could work on a building site and spend all day bending over but her bottom would be 100 percent protected from the outside world.

In other words, perfect.

Which is why it came as such a disappointment when I sought more of my ideal undies — in Napier, Gisborne, downtown Auckland and finally at the Bendon shop in Newmarket — to find that they were out of stock. It was the end of a line, no more, gone, finito.

I couldn't believe that style 14-146 had been such a fizzer. Surely there were other botties in the land like mine — in need of decent coverage but not averse to a bit of lace and the appropriate amount of Elastane.

Apparently not.

Luckily for me Ballantynes was just a phone call away. I cleaned them out of their size large Teaberrys and threw in a couple of Champagnes for good measure. And if there's one thing I can do, for the next year at least, it's hold my end up in an accident.

That Special Outfit

WHAT'S THE POINT in getting older if you don't get any wiser, I ask myself. Without the whole wise thing, you're just a wrinkly, fat version of your young, dumb self and that, quite frankly, has little appeal.

Excuse my poor form but I write this fresh from another humiliating experience in trying to find an "outfit" for a special occasion.

You might have thought I would have learned, from six thousand previous outfit-buying commando raids, that they are a one-way ticket to gloom and depression — but no, I forgot.

When the invitation arrived to the special occasion, I knew exactly what I wanted to wear.

"I'll get something long and black and spangly," I told the Ginger, who paled visibly and started to shake. "You know, quite sophisticated. Separates, perhaps, but still cocktail glamorous."

I could picture myself so clearly in this outfit. I would be gorgeous.

I would wear those very sheer, shiny, skin-coloured tights and big, high, strappy black shoes and a flowing skirt and my spangly top.

Imagine my horror when I went to the actual shops here in the real world and there wasn't so much as a single spangle to be found in a size bigger than Screw You Dolores, let alone a whole garment.

After two whole days spent — unsuccessfully — shopping, I realised that, under close scrutiny, the me I had pictured in my imaginary outfit was not, in fact, the real me but Julia Roberts.

Now, while in many respects Julia and I are so similar people get us confused, this would not very often happen — how can I put this? — in a changing room scenario.

In a changing room scenario Julia and I are not alike at all, not one little bit.

So while I was plucking clothes for Julia off the rack, I was finding them sorely lacking in the buttoning-up department when applied to my good self.

This, after two days, as you can imagine, was quite annoying/suicide-inspiring.

"You need to keep trying," the Ginger said gently, extricating the empty bottle of Malibu from my grasp as I lay in bed surrounded by used kettle-fry crisp packets. "You can't give up. You just can't."

He was right. No way was I going naked. There are laws, after all.

By eight o'clock the next morning I was on the factory floor of my favourite clothing designer, Trelise Cooper.

After begging and pleading, I was unleashed on her fabric supplies and finally found something in the most gorgeous shade of lilac. After I cried and moaned for long enough, they agreed to make it up into a suitable garment.

Problem solved. Apart from shoes. After another whole day in the shops, I found a pair the perfect style and colour.

The only problem was the size. No matter how hard I tried to make the darned things fit, they just wouldn't — as the woman in the shoe shop kept telling me as she tried to grab them and put them back in the box where they belonged.

After something of a tussle, however, she agreed I could take them on appro and see if Auckland's premier cobbler could stretch them.

"I've found a pair of shoes the right colour," I told the cobbler, "but they're too small and they really hurt. Should I buy them?"

He looked at me pityingly.

"I think you know the answer to that," he said.

New shoes, nil. Wisdom, one.

Pashminas

WHEN A FRIEND RANG me a year or so ago to say her darling husband-to-be had bought her a pashmina, I was at a loss for words.

Should you walk it or eat it, I fought the urge to ask. Should you rub cream on it or exfoliate it, I wondered. Should you roll it up and smoke it or get in and take the top down and drive it away?

I had no idea what a pashmina was.

For a while, I pretended.

"Well," I told my fianced friend, "the pashmina-exchanging drops right off once he's got that ring on your finger, I'll tell you that for nothing."

Concerned I was missing out, though, I started hounding my own poor Ginger.

"You never give me pashminas any more," I complained bitterly.

"No — but I let you read my *Auto Trader*," he answered, not particularly helpfully.

"What a lovely dog you have there," a smartly dressed lady with lots of gold jewellery said to me in the park one morning. "What sort is he?"

"Oh, he's a pashmina," I said, pretending to sneeze at the same time, in case I had it wrong.

"A what?" she asked, confused.

"A pashmina," I repeated, with a cough.

She looked at me strangely and started to back away but, as a bit of fake cough gob had caught her in the eye, I wasn't sure if this was pashmina-related or not.

Still none the wiser, I turned to my three-year-old nephew.

"If I bought you a pashmina, what would you call it?" I asked him.

"Warm and cosy," he said. "Aren't all cashmere shawls made in Nepal?"

Of course. Yes. That's right. I knew that.

Ahem.

Well, once I knew what pashminas were, I started seeing them everywhere — in magazines, in other magazines, in more magazines after that. Madonna wore one around her neck like a scarf, Calista Flockhart lived in one, Helena Christensen fashioned hers into a baby sling.

So, naturally, when I was in New York (she drops casually into the conversation) and found myself standing outside a shop dedicated entirely to layer upon layer of nothing but pashminas, I had to go in.

Armed with the knowledge that Thursday is the new Saturday and black is like, you know, I sought assistance and emerged, about four hours later, the proud owner of a shawl in the most delicate shade of pale blue.

"It's so spring," the girl in the shop had said.

"You paid *that*?" the Ginger choked some time later, looking at my credit card bill, which I hadn't had the nouse to hide in the laundry pile like I usually do. "For a grey scarf?"

There is no excuse for violence in the home, so I resisted the urge to pluck his eyes out with my fingernails and eat them and, instead, gently pointed out, while sitting on him, the difference between mucky off-white and delicate eggshell.

"It's so spring," I made him write 100 times on the pages of his car magazines, stopping only when the phone rang.

"You'll never guess what that darling man of mine has bought me now," my newly married friend trilled down the line.

Please God, let me know what she is talking about this time, I prayed.

"A poncho!"

On the other hand, sometimes you're better off not knowing.

Colour

THERE IS NO DOUBT yucky stuff starts happening to you as you get older — things sprout; things sag; things crinkle; things that oughtn't sway in the breeze. You know — like underarms.

Still, you expect these signposts to approaching old age and decay. They're no surprise. In fact, if you're clever, you start saving when you are five years old and, 40 years later, pay a nice man with fancy certificates and a series of sharp instruments to stave them off for a while.

If you're not clever, you just stop getting your eyes checked regularly and start enjoying the fuzzy sensation which comes with looking in a mirror. Sadly, I'm in the not-clever category in this and, no doubt, many more respects but, while I've been busy concentrating on the predictable saggy, crinkly things, something much more scary has crept up on me — colour. Ever since I could make out colour, I have preferred black. It makes you look thinner. It matches other black things. It makes you look thinner. It never goes out of fashion. It makes you look thinner. It is casual but sophisticated. It makes you look thinner. For as long as I can remember, my wardrobe has had so many black clothes in it, it has looked empty — the original black hole. But at the beginning of last year, in a fit of having seven weddings to go to and only one day to organise an outfit to wear to them, I bought a red dress. Suddenly, there was a gaping wound, a gash, in my clothing collection. Sure, I hyperventilated every time I saw it but I still wore it.

Then in March came the pale blue pashmina incident. So spring. And if you thought I had stopped banging on about the blasted pashmina, think again. By the time I had my poxy shawl home and ready to drape in a sophisticated fashion around my shoulders, foreign fashion editors were already declaring the whole pashmina thing "over" and suggesting they be recycled as beach towels. At that price? Over my dead body. I'll be showing off about my pashmina till they're being used as ripped-up dishrags in Third World countries, thank you very much.

Now where was I? Beach towels, indeed. Oh yes, so at this stage, my sea of black was sporting a splash of red and a dash of blue. But unable to cope with this terrible turnaround, I became panicked and decided to stop delving into the crazy world of kaleidoscopic colour. Who knew where it would end?

Just this week though, there have been three different occasions on which I have tried on 65 black things, not liked them, and gone for a more colourful option. I must have been shopping in my sleep because I now seem to have quite an array of pastel-coloured shirts. Well, two — a blue one and a mauve one. But still — pastels? What's next? Loud, flowery mumus and novelty socks? I'm scared.

"Excuuuuuuuuuse me!" the Ginger said, upon opening the mail the other night. "What is this?"

He held up a card sporting a square of pink fabric.

"Thththitha culla swutha," I mumbled.

"A what?"

"A CULLA SWUTHA."

"A WHAT?"

"IT'S A COLOUR SWATCH," I answered.

"From America?"

"It was free," I whispered, realising at the same time that sending away to foreign countries for small squares of pink was not completely normal. Still, I don't want to rush things.

Internet Shopping

I SHOULD HAVE KNOWN shopping for togs without leaving the comfort of my own tracksuit pants would have a dark side and I've found it.

How my fingers flew across the keyboard when I discovered the joy of combining one's credit card number with the many Internet websites offering on-line shopping opportunities.

Finally, a girl being whisked away for a few days to a sunny secluded beach could buy a swimming costume in perfect conditions with not a mirror below the waist to be found and no one testing her stomach-holding-in stamina by rapping on the door wanting to know how she's getting on.

Speedily, I sent off to the US for the togs which promised they could hold me in in places I didn't know stuck out. Oh, the excitement! And while I was there, I bunged a shirt and a couple of pairs of strides on the credit card as well.

"In for a penny, in for a pound!" I cried as the Ginger tried yet again to explain the finer points of decimal currency.

Imagine my horror when, two weeks later, I got a letter from customs saying they were holding my clothes prisoner until I paid a huge amount of money for their release.

All that spandex had somehow breached the official limit of $145 worth of clothes allowed into the country.

After talking to the nice man on the phone for quite a while, I established if I had worn the clothes into the country myself or had them sent in separate packages, I would not have had to pay the extra exorbitant $150.

I would still have ended up with the same amount of clothes but they would have cost me 30 percent less. Did I have that right?

"Yes," said the nice man quite quietly. "It's a bit of a flaw, really."

What would happen, I also needed to know, if the mail order clothes turned out not to be what I wanted and I sent them back?

Oh, well, it gets quite complicated then, I heard.

First, I would have to get verification from the Post Office I had sent the ill-fitting garments back to the US and then I would have to write a letter to customs explaining why my big fat butt didn't fit into those poxy yankee pants in the first place.

Then I would get my tax back — after about three weeks.

"The cheque has to come from Treasury," the nice man explained in a whisper.

Right.

"Take my package and stick it on the next plane back to the US then, will you?" I suggested sweetly. "I just can't afford to get those togs out on bail."

Well, it seems madam would have to go to the Post Office to pay for that to happen.

Using the remains of my UE maths, I worked out this would mean forking out about $40 for a pair of togs I had not yet had the pleasure of meeting to have a round-the-world trip.

Suddenly, I snapped.

"I'll tell you what," I said coldly into the phone. "How about I take my fat little thighs down to Treasury right now and expose them to the Chief High Pooh-Bah, who can then decide if it is likely I shall fit into the contents of the package I have not seen but which you are currently holding for ransom. If it is likely, I'll pay the tax then and there. If it's not, he can stamp my butt and whistle Dixie for the postage… Hello? Hello?"

Windbreakers

I'VE BEEN A BIT SHORT lately of things to worry about so it was with some relief that I read a newspaper article, e-mailed to me by a friend, that claimed normal healthy humans break wind an average of 16 times a day.

I've been under some pressure to perform ever since, I can tell you.

How many beans can a normal, healthy human eat before exploding, I wonder?

Anyway, despite upping my roughage considerably, I found myself still sadly below par. Even on a good day I was way off 16 and that's with cabbage AND muesli. Together.

After several days of depressing stomach-churning non-activity I re-read the original e-mail and discovered the point of the newspaper story was not how many emissions a day one could manage but how one might handle the more offensive emissions once they had been managed.

In short, it was about filtered underpants.

Whoever would have thought knickers could get more bizarre than the thong!

Anyway, it seems some Colorado old-timer with a particularly flatulent missus (thanks to a bowel disorder) has invented special underpants with a replaceable charcoal filter that sucks up the smell while allowing the harmless odourless gases to escape, therefore clearing the air but reducing the risk of dangerous explosions.

Apparently, he happened upon this discovery while experimenting with a gas mask. Exactly why he was experimenting with it at that end of his anatomy remains unclear.

Needless to say, he simply popped the slightly tweaked gas mask filter into the "rump" of his undies and ronked away, marvelling in the fresh, clean air that remained around him.

Then he nipped down to the Patent Office to fend off any other gas mask enthusiasts who might have made the same discovery.

The undies, said the *Denver Post* story (and I checked it out in case it was a hoax), are made from a soft airtight nylon-type fabric with elastic sewn around the waist and both legs.

This means that they are almost identical in construction to the St Mary's sporting romper of the mid 1970s.

Not surprising, then, that at a Colorado health fair the anti-ronker romper, complete with filter similar, apparently, to a woman's shoulder pad, failed to sell even one pair.

But that doesn't mean its flatulence-defending properties were over-looked. Oh no. Far from it. Once home from the fair the tyre kickers who had simply glanced at the brochures before moving on to the anti-baldness cream next door got straight onto their computers and ordered the knicks over the Net. Big time.

"What could I invent that you need special knickers for?" I asked the Ginger.

"An extra bottom?" he suggested cheerfully. "Another Tom Jones? Laxative Pringles potato chips?"

Honestly, I don't know why I bother. I get more sense out of the dog most of the time and he licks his own private parts and eats sticks.

"Well, if charcoal filters out odour," I asked the Ginger, thinking of his own trumpeting skills in the Dutch oven department, "what stops noise?"

"You could try being quiet," the great lug answered, "although you've never managed it for long in the past."

Oh, bring me a red hot poker and a pottle of honey, someone, would you?

For the next few days I worked tirelessly around the clock perfecting my own flawless invention, before presenting it with great aplomb to my beloved at bedtime.

"It looks like your old St Mary's rompers," he said, confused.

"That's right," I replied. "Now roll them up, stick them in your mouth and maybe I'll get some peace around here."

Our Four-Legged Friends

Pet-sitting

AT THE RISK of putting at least half the population off me, I am not a cat person, not by a long shot.

I find the joke about dogs having owners and cats having staff not nearly funny enough because it's so busy being true. Plus I'm allergic to them. They make my eyes run, my nose stream, my skin tingle and sometimes, if I'm really lucky, I get hives.

Which is why I can't for the life of me fathom why I agreed to house-sit a home with not one but two of the critters. Maybe it had something to do with the house's location — one block from the water in a leafy inner-Sydney suburb. Not that one needs the water when one's house has its own pool, mind. Hmmm, maybe I can fathom it after all.

To begin with, I thought if there was going to be any trouble on the pet-sitting front it would come from the dog of the house, which is the size of a Shetland pony but with a bigger head and longer hair.

One sweep of his enormous tail could take out a whole tray of cocktails (I know this for a fact) and his food bowls were the size of your average jacuzzi.

He needed to be walked twice a day even though he didn't want to and his bowels were so regular that for the first time in the history of the world, there weren't enough plastic bags in the cupboards.

In short, he was hard work. But grateful! Just looking at him made him happy. Talking to him made him delirious. Patting him had him in stitches and sitting on the floor playing with him nearly tipped him over the edge.

Plus, when you bent over to put food in his bowl, the nudge he gave your rear end could put a smile on your face for a week.

Not so his housemates, two singularly unimpressed felines.

While the dog had greeted us with much vigour and vim, the cats took one look, then slunk off, totally unimpressed.

One then went to sleep in the laundry basket while the other headed haughtily for its three-level leopard print play station. Just the sort of lair Jackie Collins would go for, were she a cat.

The next we saw of them they were sitting on our heads first thing the next morning.

When I tried to get mine off my face, it growled. Eventually I got it down to underneath my chin where it proceeded to give me a delightful scabby rash.

The next day I thought I had made a breakthrough when one of them rubbed itself against my ankles in a most endearing fashion. Then when I bent to pat it, it bit me on the leg.

I rang its owner, worried that our presence was turning it psycho.

"That's just their way of showing affection," she laughed before we were mysteriously cut off.

As the days passed, I got used to feeding the cats when they demanded it, rubbing arnica on my "affection spots" and having my face used as a pillow but when it was time to leave, I could not pretend I was going to miss them.

Which is why I nearly died of shock when I opened my suitcase back home and found one in my luggage.

Hours later the Ginger found me, shaking like a leaf and talking gibberish (no change there then) under the bed.

"It's not a cat," he said, waving the very creature at me, "it's the slippers your brother gave you for Christmas."

Upon close inspection he was right. And now I'm not a slipper person either.

Pooches

I'M SETTLING INTO the rural lifestyle for a month's residence in Ohakune quite well as it turns out. While the Ginger is at work, I troll the supermarket and video shop, chatting with the locals and organising my day's entertainment.

The dog, on the other hand, is having much more trouble adjusting.

Used to sitting in the car for hours while I dally at the deli or smoke fags and drink vodka at the back of a city aerobics class, when we first arrived in Ohakune, he couldn't get used to the great outdoors.

He took to lying, shaking, on his custom-built doggy divan while, outside, the other animals in the neighbourhood did their usual Ohakune animal stuff.

For example, just the other day, I looked out the window and there was a huge stag lying on the lawn.

This didn't surprise me too much because, every now and then, I wake up and there's a horse in our backyard. The stag, however, on closer inspection, turned out to be an enormous canine chewing on a pair of antlers.

This started quite a debate between myself and my own pooch, who had taken to lying in front of the fire with a box of chocolates and a romantic novel.

Question number one — where was the rest of that deer?

Question number two — what was that dog going to want for dessert?

To my surprise, our city dog eventually decided to bounce next door and make friends with his neighbour — at least, I think that's what it means when the big dog picks the little dog up by its neck and shakes it around a bit.

Before I knew it, our Kerry blue terrier was making friends with every hound in the neighbourhood until it became quite clear that, an only pet for too long, he had fallen in with a bad crowd.

He started skulking around in a sulky fashion and growling all the time before gambolling around various alpine gardens with a gang of naughty mutts in tow. I sat at the window fearful that at any moment I would see him running along the street with a string of sausages in his mouth and an angry butcher chasing him.

For a while, I tried talking to him about not giving in to peer pressure but, what with only having a brain the size of a walnut and all, he seemed to prefer licking the soles of my shoes to taking in my advice on survival skills.

All hell broke loose when the Ginger came home and found him lolling on the sofa with his girlfriend from up the road, though. While I'd given up strict parenting in the interests of a peaceful household, the Ginger wasn't having a bar of it.

After much shooing and yelling and gibes about cheap tarts who don't know when to go home, the little bitch slunk off in the direction of somewhere else, but surprised us both by returning in the dead of night, underneath our house, directly below our bed, in fact — where she proceeded to bark up a storm for several hours.

Finally, again in the interests of a peaceful household, I gathered all the neighbourhood mutts together and calmly explained not only does our dog get his hair cut but that I drive him to Auckland and pay $50 for the privilege.

Haven't seen hide nor hair of them since.

Every Home Should Have One

Gingers

"WHY IS IT we so love to make fun of gingers?" I wondered idly the other day, as I was packing up my kit of Ginger-taunting material.

This included: a postcard, featuring a little red-headed boy being threatened with a lifetime at the "home for unwanted ginger children" (should the waiting list ever abate); the English newspaper headline "Ginger No Friends", with pictures of Fergie and Cilla Black; and the guaranteed-to-split-your-sides "I'll See You, Jimmy" hat, bought in Scotland.

This is a 100 percent synthetic tartan hat, with truly foul fake orange hair attached around the bottom. Put it on a brunette or a blonde and it is mildly amusing. Place it on the pate of a bona fide brickhead and it will have even the most dour of audiences wetting themselves within moments. It's a complexion thing, you see.

This I know because, as you may have gathered, I have my own personal ginger on whom to test these taunts — and very good he is about it, too.

Although he did put a stop to the habit I got into of tooting the horn — the way Alfa Romeo drivers might honk at each other — at similarly-hued heads walking along the street. Once I'd honked, I'd slow down and wave at them. "Look!" I'd cry in excitement. "Another ginger!"

He may have put the kibosh on that but mostly he bears the ginger jibes as proudly as his head of flaming hair — only because, he foolishly confided in me one day, he knows deep down he isn't really ginger.

Looking at him, you might wonder how he reached that conclusion. Once I stopped slapping my thigh and holding my sides, I, too, pointed this out to him.

But then he produced a snapshot of himself as a nipper and — my goodness — a carrot should be so lucky. Apparently, the poor creature suffered a childhood full of "Hello, Carrot Top! Where did you get that hair from then? The milkman, eh?"

Young Ginger found it particularly annoying that carrot tops are, in fact, green.

But inaccurate comparisons with vegetables were nothing compared to endless rounds of the catchy jingle associated with a popular biscuit of the time. You know the one — it's so spicey and made from old English recipe. You can ask for it by name — but, in our house, it's best not to mention it at all.

Anyway, so advancing years have dulled the glow of the Ginger's once-fluorescent orange orb enough for him to feel ginger jibes are not really aimed at him — which must be why he still looks so happy (relatively) to see me. Plus, he knows what a huge soft spot I have for the ginger folk.

I attempted having ginger hair myself once — but having a small gin-fest with my flatmates first turned out to be not such a good idea. We all woke in the morning with various shades of red on our heads — mine being the least attractive and the most brittle.

Eventually, I went to the hairdressers for a patch-up but they could never quite match the shade I'd concocted myself — a shade which became known as my "gin-bottle ginger" — and which took nearly two years to grow out.

Somehow, it seemed easier to get a ginger husband than to go through all that again and, should he go bald, there's always the "Jimmy" hat ...

Baldness

I WAS WATCHING the Ginger munch his way through a curry the other night, which is something I often do when there's nothing good on the telly.

Call me strange but, in my opinion, watching a man sweat while he eats is every bit as entertaining as perving at a bunch of half-wits getting up each other's noses on a desert island somewhere.

On this occasion, though, I suddenly felt the cold fist of fear clench around my heart. Okay, so it could have been my arteries hardening (damn those Pringles) but I was pretty sure it was panic.

According to my calculations, taking into account it was a medium, not a hot, curry and that the humidity was at a moderate level, the Ginger was fitting more beads of sweat on his forehead than usual.

This could mean only one thing. There was more of his forehead there than usual.

And this could mean only one thing — a receding hairline.

Snatching the remains of his vindaloo away from him, I lurched at the poor creature with the special tape measure I keep about my person at all times for instances such as this one.

Indeed, it appeared his hairline was moving back away from his face at a rate of about one thousandth of a millimetre per 30 years.

Disaster. It's a well-known fact, where I come from anyway, there is only one thing worse than a Ginger with a full head of hair — and that is a bald one.

Me, I don't care too much for the current trend in male baldness.

Sure, it keeps grey at bay and it allows the small glimmer of possibility that maybe you shaved all your hair off just because you wanted to, not because it was upping sticks and leaving you anyway.

But to me, all bald men look the same. You know, like giant new-born babies — only talking more rubbish.

So should the Ginger join their ranks, I would have trouble picking him out in a crowd and I can only imagine what sort of trouble would ensue.

Checking a large group of males for their natural hair colour should it not be apparent from their heads could get a girl into all sorts of trouble. And put her off her lunch to boot.

"You're only jealous," the Ginger said, slapping me off with a piece of naan bread, "because you could never be bald."

He's right. I have totally the wrong-shaped head.

Without hair, I would look like I had been slammed backwards into a concrete wall. Honestly, I must be storing a lot of brains in my neck because there's not much space in my head.

Also I couldn't live in a world without trips to the hairdresser. How would I know whose facelifts have gone horribly wrong? Whose husband is for the high jump? Who's on the cover of *Hello* magazine?

"If we were both bald," the Ginger continued, "think of the money we'd save."

Yeah, like his seven bucks fifty a month is going to get us a retirement chateau in the south of France.

My fiscal commitment to hair products, however, should it be redirected, could probably get us a time share on the Gold Coast without too much trouble.

Oh, what the heck. Let the Ginger go bald. By the time he's reached official badger status, I'll be able to pick him out of a crowd by his nose hair anyway.

Valentines

LIKE MOST MEN, the Ginger does not have a romantic bone in his body. In fact, after years of extensive searching, I don't think he has any bones at all.

Sometimes there's evidence of a spine but it never seems to last for long. And sure, there's an appendage he might personally consider romantic but he might also find I would not entirely agree with him on that.

Mind you, we are talking about a man who celebrates Valentine's Day by going to the local smorgasbord restaurant — by himself — and eating his own body weight in ham-off-the-bone and chocolate eclairs.

"It's not about piling your plate with enough food to feed a family of four," I tried explaining to him this year. "In fact, it's not actually about food."

"Huh?" his face crumpled into a confused expression and the light went out in his eyes. Then I realised I was not actually looking at the Ginger but the vacuous fluffy toy I stuff my PJs into.

I make this mistake quite often. Can't think why. Husbands keep their PJs on the outside.

"It's about expressing love and affection to your sweetheart," I continued when I tracked him down. "It's about romance and mystery."

"Huh?" he said again, his face crumpling into a confused expression and the light going out in his eyes. I checked his back for a zip but there wasn't one. It was him all right.

"It's your chance to show me how much you worship the ground I float above, you great galah!" I shrieked. "Just what is it about Valentine's Day that you don't understand?"

He blinked uncomprehendingly at me. "Why we have it," he answered. "That's what I don't understand."

Saints preserve us; does he not watch TV commercials?

"We have it," I explained in a cool and superior fashion,

"because back in the third century the very, very, very famous St Valentine, possibly the most famous saint of them all, in fact, was out one day, probably on a horse, a big white one, when..." To be honest, I suddenly found myself hazy on the details.

"When what?" the Ginger asked, a dull light returning to his peepers.

"When the postman delivered to his letterbox — a letterbox of the medieval variety, that is — a card bearing an anonymous message from a saucy wench.

"And so," I finished with a great flourish, "began the grand tradition of anonymous card-sending on St Valentine's Day."

In retrospect, it didn't really sound like a monumental enough event to have a day named after it.

"And then came three wise men," I added as an afterthought, "bearing Paris perfume, Rose's chocolates and small, very sparkly ear adornments."

"For St Valentine?" the Ginger asked. "What? He was gay?"

Can't work out what "pull" means on a door but can pick holes in a story from 40 paces. You wouldn't credit it.

"They were WISE men, doofus," I snapped. "They were bringing the gifts for St Valentine to give to his sweetheart."

"His anonymous sweetheart? The one he didn't know the name nor, presumably, the address of?"

I had to admit, he had me. What's a saint doing accepting soft porn from a nameless tart anyway? Let alone gifts from three gay stalkers. It's not right.

"Come on," the Ginger said gently. "Why don't you just sit down and I'll light a few candles and cook you a lovely dinner and give you a back rub like I do every night."

True, he's not much of a one for an occasion and you can't stuff your jammies in him but he has his uses, bless him.

Slavery

THINGS HAVE BEEN a bit slow on the Ginger's work front lately, which I was certain would put a strain on our relationship. I rely on him going to work, you see, so I can continue to do whatever it is I do all day, which isn't actually a job but takes about eight hours anyway.

So when it appeared he was going to be at home for a while without gainful employment, I admit I was less than thrilled.

I work from home after all and I have routines, you know, systems, schedules put in place for specific reasons which shouldn't be tampered with.

I'm a creative person. I need space. I need harmony. I need quiet. I need to sit down with a bag of cashews for a spot of *Oprah* to renew my spirit sometimes. And if my spirit gets too renewed, I need to watch *EastEnders* as well to get it back on an even keel.

I didn't think I wanted a husband lying around, cluttering up the house and interrupting this creative process. What if he discovered how much time I spent talking to my friends on the phone and reading joke e-mails?

Within hours, however, I realised having him constantly hovering around in the background was not altogether a bad situation. In fact, it was far from it.

Not used to so much time without someone barking orders at him, the Ginger, I quickly discovered, responded infeasibly well to instruction. Before I knew it, he was bringing me the breakfast of my choice in bed and making my lunch and dinner to boot.

Over the next six weeks, he revamped the garden, spring-cleaned the house, tidied the shed and re-organised our sock drawers, matching them up and throwing out the singles. My spirit started renewing itself without any intervention. "Need anything dry-cleaned?" the Ginger asked on his way out the door one day to pick up the boots he was getting re-soled for me.

He single-handedly rejuvenated my wardrobe by finding a man to dye black all the clothes I have bought in other colours and never wear.

He streamlined my home office so I wouldn't get mad and throw large clumps of annoying paperwork across the room.

My only complaint would be that he seemed to run out of steam about 10 at night. But I didn't feel I could hold that against him so I agreed he should just do light housework such as dusting and darning until midnight.

It came as a dreadful shock when he announced his days as my slave were over.

"But why would you want to go out and get a real job when you can stay at home all day and look after me?" I sobbed, clinging to his legs as he left the house to go to his new job.

"Can't think," he said, poking at me with a stick so he could close the car door. "Must dash."

"What's the job, anyway?" I cried as he backed down the drive.

"Don't know. Didn't ask," he shouted out the window as he accelerated away at speed.

Yesterday I was reduced to ringing him while he was in a meeting to find out how our can opener works.

"They burned their bras for this?" his exasperated voice came down the phone. "The sisterhood must be so proud." I think I know what he was getting at. Maybe a lady-in-waiting would be better.

Camping

EVERY NOW AND THEN the Ginger says something that makes me remember he really is from a different planet and should probably be cut up into tiny pieces for science experiments.

Twice this week I have rung the university and offered his body parts for research. Surely I'm keeping someone from winning the Nobel Prize by hogging the poor creature's great big empty head to myself. What if it turns out the gas he keeps in the space where his brain should be could cure cancer or fuel rocket ships?

First, he asks me how a mascara wand can make your eyelashes 30 percent longer.

The great galah, still not quite right in the head after an eight-hour marathon stretch watching the Bathhurst motor racing on TV, had become confused during a commercial break.

When a model-turned-actress sauntered on to the screen and informed him her wand could increase the length of her lashes by a third, he believed her.

Really, the cosmetic giants would make a whole lot more money if they aimed all their advertising at gormless males.

Talk about gullible. I had to explain to poor Ginge it wasn't really THAT sort of a wand and, if he thought about it hard enough, I was sure he would work out that nothing can make eyelashes longer except more eyelashes, the next size up.

Then blow me down if he doesn't suggest we go camping.

Well, you can imagine the action in my epiglottis. Choking didn't seem like a big enough response so instead I collapsed in a dead faint.

When I came to, the wretched man was untangling our collection of mouldy old tents and other outdoor paraphernalia.

Gasping for breath, I crawled across the floor and collapsed at his feet. Ignoring me, he started tinkering with those nasty aluminium pots that fit inside each other and checking that all the knives and forks and spoons were correctly attached.

"Did you learn nothing from our last camping trip?" I cried in anguish. "Nothing?"

He searched his brain for the correct answer but, as previously discussed, couldn't find it. "No," he said.

Now, I wouldn't consider myself someone who insists on fancy hotels or the best of home comforts. All I really ask for is a comfy bed and a flushing toilet. These, however, were two elements conspicuously absent during our last camping trip.

Every night we would start off with a fully inflated air mattress, only to wake up some time later to the whistling of oxygen escaping past our ears as our bones made their way towards the hard, rocky ground.

No amount of puncture kits could save us. We were getting through approximately one air bed every night at a cost of something in the vicinity of staying in a motel, yet still we had to bathe in shared facilities and cook on a primus.

One night I awoke, a twig sticking into my kidneys, to realise that not only could I hear the Ginger snoring but the man in the tent next door and the man in the tent next to him, too.

Over a breakfast of warm milk and muesli, infiltrated by wild animals who had left raisin-like pellets behind them during the night, I explained to my husband that he had better take me home or I would have to stick tent pegs up his nose and, once the matches dried out, set fire to him.

Reminding him of all this, he seemed totally mystified.

That's the thing about having a brain so small it's barely even there — you're very rarely emotionally scarred by dreadful events from your past.

Looking at his great huge eyes rolling dolefully around in his head, I felt my resolve weaken, bless him.

"Oh, all right then," I said crossly. "You'd better bring one of those wands, though. Maybe we can make the tent bigger and the long drop deeper."

House-sitting

IT'S BEEN A lifelong goal of mine to be permanently on holiday. Although to be perfectly honest, I'm not having a great deal of success. The problem is, of course, not winning Lotto, not even once, or coming second for that matter, which puts five-star vacationing at a distinct disadvantage.

As previously discussed, the only sort of holiday I can actually afford is one that involves a tent, millions of tiny insects all thirsting for my blood, sausages so charred they make sticks taste nourishing and long periods of not wanting to talk to the Ginger. On that subject (the husband, not the snarlers), I must digress and you will soon see why.

It's just that lately I have had quite a few people asking me what the Ginger thinks about being belittled so mercilessly within the confines of this column. Does he not object to being ridiculed for having a head that's totally devoid of brain and big and red and round to boot, they ask?

Well, I am going to let you in on a little secret. Although I have trained the poor creature up brilliantly in most respects, there are some areas over which I still have no control, no matter how hard I try.

Every now and then, for example, he leaves the loo seat up. Occasionally he doesn't replace the toilet roll. Once he even brought me my breakfast in bed before I was properly awake — incredible.

Anyway, it has come to my attention that the great lug does not read this column. Oh, he pretends to. He looks at the picture all right but then, quite slyly for him, he notes just the heading and the ending.

This way if I put him on the spot, he has an answer or two to cling to before I get the frying pan out and direct it at his cranium. This week, for example, if I ask him what I'm going on about in these very pages he will cheerfully say, "House-sitting, isn't it? Round-the-clock room service — very funny."

This bit in the middle that you're reading now? About how his brain was sucked out of his ear by a guinea pig when he was at kindergarten and, despite monitoring the little rodent's droppings for weeks, never showed up again? Not a clue.

Admittedly he gets a bit mystified when total strangers, usually grey-haired ladies with kindly expressions, come up to him in supermarkets and tell him what a love he is for putting up with it all. All I do then, though, is just tell him there are a lot of confused old crazies out there and most of them are grey-haired ladies with kindly expressions and he's happy again, bless him.

The point is, you don't need to feel sorry for him because what he doesn't know won't hurt him and even with what he does know, it's easy enough to confuse him so that he goes back to not knowing fairly quickly and without too much bother.

That said, it's time to return to the subject of my newest holiday scam.

It's called house-sitting. Sure you don't go far but the surroundings are different and the cost is negligible.

We are currently house-sitting a lovely seaside apartment not half an hour away from where we live, also at the sea.

But a change is as good as a rest, don't they say? Plus, if I play my cards right with the Ginger, I can generally guarantee round-the-clock room service.

The Crappy Wanderer

Moving

WHEN IT COMES to packing up and moving away, my advice is don't.

I'm in the middle of it as we speak and, I can tell you, there is nothing more likely to propel you into the crankiest mood of the millennium than wrapping up all the horrible things you'd forgotten you even had and transporting them at great cost to a different location.

Luckily, I have someone to blame — the Ginger. Had he not gone and got himself a job on *Lord of the Rings*, along with all the other very tall, very short or very... oh, I don't know... ginger people in the world, then we would still be sitting somewhere which wasn't surrounded entirely by cardboard boxes.

As it is, he has been summonsed to Hobbitville — although not, as I may have suggested, for reasons to do with being of a ruddy complexion but because of a huge array of other highly-honed skills. (Mental note — must ask husband what he actually does.)

As his faithful companion, I must go with him, which means abandoning Auckland for Wellington. But not without quite a lot of "The sacrifices I make" and "You owe me big-time now, buster" and "What about all the couples who live apart and still make it work?" first, of course.

Hence, I was dispatched to the capital on an advance mission to go flat-hunting.

As someone who lived in Wellington from the age of 10 and has returned there on many occasions over the years to go flat-hunting, I cannot express how depressing it was to be doing it again, at the age of 37.

In one near-horrible "To Let" incident, I actually rang up and enquired about a sunny, two-bedroom rear flat with sleep-out which, it turns out, I flatted in once before — in 1981.

Then, I bumped into an old high school friend on the street, who just couldn't believe I was still sporting the same hair-do.

"I'll be back at St Mary's, writing lines after school, at this rate," I sobbed down the phone to the Ginger. "I'll be living at home with Mum and wagging piano lessons," I continued. "The only contact I'll have with you is a quick fag down behind Rutherford House, before the 3.33 to Johnsonville."

Annoyingly enough, he warmed to this possibility, before attempting to appease me with the suggestion I might try looking for a house with a spa pool to cheer me up.

"Spa pool?" I shrieked, turning suddenly nasty — the way I like to do. "Well, when I find something which doesn't have a thousand steps, mouldy walls, a wind-chill factor of -15 degrees Celsius and no off-street parking, I'll start concentrating on the Jacuzzi, shall I?"

Letting agents the city over were quick to point out Wellington rentals are every bit as expensive, if not more so, than Auckland ones, which, at first, I didn't believe.

"You want $500 a week for a shoebox in Mount Victoria?" I chortled. "*You* should be paying *me*."

Strangely, this attitude did nothing for my flat-hunting and no amount of ranting about the calibre of my person would get them to open the door again.

Still, just before my departure, I found the perfect spot. Brand-spanking new, dead-flat section, pots of coffee, loads of storage, plenty of parking.

Could probably live there rent-free and unnoticed for quite a while. Bit noisy. Very close interest in aviation essential.

The Road Trip

A KEEN DRIVER myself, it was with relish I loaded up the dog and the contents of our kitchen cupboards for a pre-move delivery to the new home in Wellington, which I'd organised over the phone but had yet to see.

To avoid the trek from Auckland being too quiet, I also loaded up a friend, who was about to start a new job as a tour director on a luxury coach line.

"If you have any queries at all, just ask me," he rehearsed, as we got into the car. "What? No toilet?"

Usually, if I'm doing the eight-hour drive from Auckland to Wellington, it's with the Ginger and we spend most of the time playing "Black Dog, White Horse, Red Roof". First one to spot all three in that order wins — usually me, because I'm not driving and can swivel my head around and spy things better.

In other words, I cheat.

If I'm on my own, however, I spend most of the eight hours wondering what it is you can eat on a road trip which won't clog up your arteries by the time you get to Tokoroa — or extend your waistband beyond reasonable measure.

My companion, however, being of the "eat-all-you-like-never-put-on-a-gram" persuasion, had no time at all for this and had eaten my entire lentil sandwich collection by the time we got to the end of his driveway and made us stop just moments later for crisps and boiled sweets as well.

"On our left, we have some lovely trees," he intoned, on the motorway south. "Must find out more about those."

"And, on our right," he continued, a few kilometres further, "some lovely looking buildings where I think they sell horses. Must find out more about those, too."

His helpful commentary kept me from worrying about what I was going to find to eat which wouldn't come in a pastry case or be a lamington — but, by Taupo, I was rumbling.

"On our right, we have pizza to go and, on our left, the golden arches," my tour director informed me. "In the middle, we have a lovely delicatessen but no drive-through."

The quick option was not going to be the healthy option and I really couldn't wait, so golden arches it was. Luckily, I remembered if you drive fast enough while eating this sort of food, the kilojoules cannot cling and, if you open the windows as well, they get sucked into thin air without attaching themselves to any part of you.

"On our left, we have carrot cake and coffee," my director informed me in an authoritative tone at Taihape.

"Beware, low-flying tea-rooms," he warned, as we approached Mangaweka where your sausage rolls and other bite-sized snacks come inside a DC3.

"On our right the local police station," he pointed out at Bulls. "Watch out or the 'consta-bull' will get you."

"Ice-cream and cheese — what a lovely combination," he cried, as we passed Lindale, on the Kapiti Coast.

"This is your place?" he asked, as we stared up the driveway to the Wellington flat I'd arranged, sight unseen.

"On your left, you have Middle Eastern takeaways, pizzas and a burger bar," he said, looking at me pityingly. "And, on your right, fish and chips, Chinese takeaways and a liquor store. Good luck!"

Moving Again

I AM ABSOLUTELY POSITIVE that at some stage in the past two years, I issued a decree that if I ever talked about moving again I was to be soundly slapped.

Joan Collins, I recall, said the same thing about getting married. So as she honeymoons with husband number five, I find myself once again living in Queenstown.

One minute life was trotting along as normal at our Auckland west coast hideaway, the next the Ginger was rambling on about monsters in a lake and the Deep South.

Nonsensical ramblings are nothing new in our house so I simply ignored him. However, a week or so ago I got home and there was a note saying that, as discussed (obviously not with me), he had gone to Queenstown to work on a film about a monster in a lake. All I had to do, the note said, was pack up the car and he would see me down there.

He had travelled by air, a rather uncomplicated journey involving one and a half hours of his time and free drinks. I, on the other hand, was to take the road option, involving three days' driving, a ferry crossing and my own bodyweight in roadside snacks.

Before I hit the road for the big trek though, I had a frenetic day of errands to be accomplished. I was packed to the gunnels but first I had to go and pick up the dog from the South Auckland boot camp where he had been learning to appreciate cats. Once I had him, I had to take the car back to the mechanic because the back window kept falling down, I had to take my winter shoes to get fixed, I had drycleaning to drop off, clothes to be delivered to the Salvation Army, a lunch date with the friend looking after our house, business at the bank and the Post Office — and that was just the first part of the list.

Not on the list was having a blow-out in the middle of the South Auckland countryside.

Luckily for me, the blow-out happened right on the doorstep

of a country service station, where a nice man came straight out and fixed the whole thing for the princely sum of 15 bucks.

Unluckily for me, the NEXT blow-out happened on the Grafton Road off-ramp and I had to limp up to bustling Symonds St in the city before the blasted vehicle collapsed at the side of the road next to the traffic lights.

"Jeez, lady, you really rooted your car, eh?" a goofy student in jeans that were falling off his pathetic excuse for hips guffawed. One small tug and I could have exposed his pale pimply bottom to the world. Then who'd be laughing, eh?

Two hours later the mechanic who had been responsible for "fixing" the tyres just days before turned up, red in the face and bearing a Firestone man.

"Your husband said I had to come and get you straight away," the mechanic said.

This surprised me not at all as I had just rung my husband and told him I was pushing his car and his dog into the harbour and going straight to the airport to catch a plane for the Congo.

"I want to make sure you get to Queenstown safely," the mechanic said, wiping the sweat off his brow and waving goodbye a further hour later.

"I really don't want to hear from your husband ever again."

A husband who can strike such fear into the heart of an auto repairman? Easily worth a three-day drive. Joan should be so lucky.

Elbows, knees and Whoops-a-daisy

Behinds

"FROM THIS ANGLE," my beach buddy squinted up at me, "did you realise you have absolutely no bum?"

Excuse me, but a moment's silence seems appropriate.

"But I've written a whole book about having a BIG bum," I gasped, all aquiver.

"Well, you should have written it about your upper arms," she said, before rolling over and falling asleep.

Yeah, whatever, but before that was the bit about not having a big bum, I thought, and that's the bit I like.

Ever since the days of high school regulation rompers, I've been worried about that overgrown jiggly peach which follows me wherever I go. And I suspect there are plenty of others out there who share similar concerns — about their own bums, thank you very much, not mine.

For example, hands up who never buys anything for their top half which stops above the thighs. Step forward if you've put your neck out passing your reflection in a shop window. Show me the bruise where you've banged your head trying to check out your behind while refusing to leave the cubicle at the jeans shop.

And remember the day you were thrown out of *9 1/2 Weeks* for shouting, "Yes, but WHAT SIZE heart-shaped ass do you love?" at Mickey Rourke. Or was that just me?

The point is, we don't want to clog up a whole new millennium with bad feelings about our bottom lines. Never mind that your beach buddy slips into a daiquiri-induced coma just seconds after commenting on the firmness of your cheeks. Who cares that her already double vision was further blurred by your thighs which, without so much as a by-your-leave, are keeping the memory of Zinzan Brooke alive by recreating his proportions, only wobblier.

It doesn't matter that your butt sometimes speaks to you in words which only you can hear, such as, "I'm feeling out of whack on the left-hand side. How about a white chocolate Magnum?" And why worry that it took 17 years of step aerobics before your jelly-like botty pulled itself together?

It's time we started only taking notice of the nice things people say about us, especially below the belt — no matter what level of drunken torpor they're in at the time.

So the next time someone attacks your backside with a pea-shooter and counts the ripples out loud, wait until they've finished and congratulate them on their mathematical prowess. "And with those eyes so close together — well done!" Or take a moment to think of someone with a much, much fatter butt than your own and silently say, "Thanks, love. I feel better about mine now."

Anyway, I'd better go as I have a team of scientists working around the clock in my basement on the design of an outfit for New Year's Eve which will reveal only the still-dyed bits of my hair and, from certain angles, my rear.

So far it's black, has lots of straps and involves contortions I'm not up for to get into but, with the right combination of hallucinogenic drugs, vodka and home-made pikelets, I'm sure the boffins can do better.

Hair Removal

"LOOK AT THOSE ROOTS," I gasped at myself in the mirror, which in itself was frightening, because, like most people, I pull a special face to look in the mirror and it doesn't involve gasping.

In fact, it doesn't involve any movement at all apart from a bit of sucking-in, a lot of eyebrow-raising, poor lighting and a chin angle worked out on computers by men with colour-coded ballpoints in their pockets. But really, the root rot at my temples was a sight to behold.

Who knew when my mother told me if you pull out one grey hair, 10 come to its funeral, she was actually telling the truth?

There's only one thing I can do about the sad lack of "natural mahogany/chestnut" on my head, I thought, and that's wear a hat.

True, not in itself a bad thing but, combined with the full-length trousers forced on me by lack of leg waxing, long sleeves brought about by armpit extrusions and temperatures of up to 30 degrees Celsius — excuse me, when exactly did hair take over the world?

Honestly, if I'm not washing, conditioning, moisturising, bleaching and colouring it, I'm lasering, shaving, waxing, plucking or covering it. It's practically a full-time job.

If yashmaks were even remotely fashionable... actually, don't get me started on lip hair. I'll be forced to recount the Bleached Ginger Handlebar Disaster of 1997 and, trust me, you don't want to go there.

Anyway, sick of overheating, fainting and having no one remotely good-looking give me mouth-to-mouth, I decided to make time in my busy depilatory schedule for an overdue visit to the waxing chamber.

"But no," a friend I exposed my pins to on the way cried.

"What you need for that veritable forest on your legs is my new-fangled, plug-in thing which rips the hairs out with no pain whatsoever."

So stunned was I by the "veritable forest" business, I failed to notice the mutual exclusivity of "rips the hairs out" and "no pain whatsoever".

Next thing I know, we're in the bedroom wrenching follicles from my shin like there's no tomorrow, which is not a scene you want to think about for long or have your husband walk in on.

The verdict? He's got brains, that Mr Braun, but his coffee machines sure hurt less than his Silk Epil Super Softs. Does the Super Soft, in turn, hurt less than your conventionally eye-watering wax-off, though?

Half an hour later, the experiment complete and the remaining shin professionally denuded in the usual excruciating fashion, the answer was, "Yes". Plus the new-fangled, plug-in thing can be employed in the privacy of your own home, so it doesn't matter if your knickers are tatty.

My big job this week, then, is to watch my leg hair grow, flow-chart the results and then rush to calculate which removal system is better before the title of Person Most Likely To Be Told To "Get a Life" comes up for grabs.

I know, I know — being hairy isn't the worst thing in the world. It's just that being asked to play the yeti in *The X-Files* does get creepy after a while.

The Fat Farm

DAY ONE: Darlings! Here I am in Queensland, ready for a week of munching mung beans and knitting my own sandals at Camp Eden Health Resort. All I have to go without is meat, alcohol, salt, sugar, coffee, tea, milk, cheese, mind-expanding drugs and fags — and it's not like I'm dependent on any of those.

I expect I shall just float through the week on a cloud of inner peace and purity and be rattling around in my slacks by the end of it all.

However, I did have a slight hiccup upon entry. The presence of airline French toast, bacon and maple syrup was detected on my breath but a quick search revealed no other signs of airline food so I was admitted.

Goodness, I don't know how those Australian scales work — they must pop an extra zero on the end. And the tape measures across the Tasman sure are out of whack.

Day two: Got a terrible fright when the bell clanged at 5.45am for tai chi on the lawn. I was having the best dream ever about toad-in-the-hole. Managed to pull my groin, put my back out and poke myself in the eye with a stick — and that was just putting my shoes on.

Got sent to the back of the lawn for suggesting if we sped the tai chi up, we could all be at the breakfast table sooner. Although typical of the spirit of Sarah-Kate Lynch, this is apparently contrary to the spirit of tai chi.

Breakfast is a one-kilometre walk away but the fact it's a smorgasbord keeps me trekking through the rain forest at a cracking pace. I mightn't be good at beach volleyball but I come into my own at the buffet.

Day three: Some campers are having trouble coping without coffee — but not me. Goodness, is that the time? I must have dozed off.

Got all excited at the tea table last night when I clapped eyes on the large bowl of chilli con carne my meat radar had earlier detected from the top of a hill three kilometres away. Imagine my dismay when it turned out to be chilli non carne.

Not that going without meat has been a problem. I've never strictly been just a meat-eater. I've always been vegetarian as well.

Day four: Whoever had the idea of putting the mess hall at the top of the hill and everything else at the bottom was a mean and probably terribly thin person. And whoever called it sunny Queensland? For this much rain, I could have gone to Hokitika.

Being pure sure gives you one hell of a headache and the inner peace is clogging up my bowels something wicked.

Day five: Send steak.

Day six: You know, I'm over the worst of it. In fact, I think a girl could get used to this lifestyle.

Tai chi in the early dawn, a walk, breakfast, some yoga, a bit of a massage, a facial, lunch, a swim in the pool, a cooking class, dinner and sleep.

No kids, no work, no phones, no traffic jams, no jams, no sugar, no salt, no coffee, no alcohol and no meat — except fish on Tuesdays.

Day seven: Never mind your head-phones, I'll have the chicken and the chardonnay, thank you.

Tanning

FOR A SUN-WORSHIPPER like myself, it's been very hard coming to terms with the fact it's no longer cool to have a tan. I mean it's just so 20th century.

And, while I can appreciate why being pale and interesting is in, I still can't get past the fact brown legs look thinner than white ones. I'm trying to brainwash myself out of this theory but it's a major psychological shift which may eventually require therapy. It took me ages to train my pale Irish skin into changing colour come the summer in the first place.

When our family moved, when we were little, from Dunedin to Auckland, how we delighted in spending 10- to 12-hour stretches at the beach. How we marvelled as our skin turned beetroot and bubbled before our very eyes. How we fought over who had the most blisters; who needed the most soothing lotion.

When we moved to Wellington, the sun wasn't quite such an issue, which provided the perfect training ground for me to implement a strict tanning regime. For two years, I embarked on a relentless programme of covering myself with creams which smelled of coconut and baking myself in the sun — each day for a little longer than the day before.

Eventually — after dedicating only 6598 hours of my life each year — I could almost be considered, in poor lighting, for at least two weeks of the year, to be olive-skinned. I could then lie in a row with my girlfriends for hours, lathered in baby oil, glistening in the sunshine, lacking only a non-stick surface and some garlic and onion.

And, when you peeled, oh, the delight! The new generation knows nothing of the pleasure of pulling sheets of dead skin off the backs of perfect strangers.

Nowadays, I am, of course, aware having legs which seem thinner than they are is no match for dying of skin cancer but I still fight a constant battle with myself to not run outside and get my kit off the moment the sun comes out. I guess it's a little easier since my neighbours got that petition going but, still, the urge is there.

Now, tanners like myself have to sunbathe in secret. A disguise is out of the question. I know, because I tried it. But, by the time you're finished camouflaging yourself as a 60-year-old Greek man, there's not a lot of skin left to expose.

Even in the privacy of my own backyard, I have to trick my Ginger husband into believing I'm toiling in the garden, rather than sauteing myself. How he thinks I can toil from the reclining position on a sun lounger I don't know and I'm not going to ask, because I'm not stupid — I'm beige.

I've also heard some naturally tanned folk now tell fibs about how they got that way. "Oh, it's a fabulous, new, spray-on product from Guerlauderique," they insist. "You can buy it on the Net."

Yet, a close inspection of legs and arms will reveal not one single streak or tell-tale splodge, which any real faketanner knows goes hand in hand with this form of browning.

Is that rain clearing up? Must dash — I swear I saw a patch of blue sky. Pass the SPF15 and the hoe, would you?

Hair

I DON'T KNOW WHY I do it. It's sad really. You would think, by now, I would have learned. But no.

"I'd like my hair cut like this," I said to the hairdresser, pulling a page ripped from a magazine out of my bag.

She looked at the little twiglet in the picture with her spunky, short hairstyle clipped to one side with something from Tiffany's. And then she looked at me.

Back at the spunky twiglet. Back at me.

"Don't go there, Sarah-Kate," she finally said, scrunching the page into a ball and throwing it with expert dexterity into a bin in the little room out the back.

She'd been there before. But then so had I.

Like much of the world, I attempted Farrah Fawcett's outward flick as a schoolgirl but didn't have the length or the curling tongs and so ended up with a sad, frizzy sort of pageboy.

The shaggy came next but was not a good look — unless you like being confused with the missing extra brother no one knew your family had.

The black and white checks on the back of my head? Don't even get me started on that one. All I can say is, if your hairdresser ever asks you what your favourite shape is, think carefully before you answer. It may not just be small talk.

Is it any wonder then that I have spent nearly two decades with what is basically the same brown bob?

Several times, in a bid to overhaul my tired image, I have tried taking pictures of the young Elizabeth Taylor to the hair salon with me.

"I can make you look like she does NOW," one young hopeful said doubtfully before I was forced to stick velcro rollers to the hairs on her arms and smack her botty with a hairbrush.

Of course, one problem with taking a picture of someone gorgeous to the hairdresser's is you don't really just want their hair — you want the cheekbones, the waist measurement, the fancy house, the big car, the free stuff famous people get sent, the therapy, the lot.

Now my hairdresser is pretty good but I'm picking her facial reconstruction and liposuction skills are what let her down on the turning-customers-into-Meg-Ryan front.

For all I know, Meg Ryan takes a picture of Julia Roberts to the hairdresser and says, "I want to look like her. Can you make me look like her?"

Or perhaps she just plops down in the chair and says, "Do whatever you want. It really doesn't matter. It'll look fabulous anyway. (Sigh!)"

It would be too cruel if there was only one person in the world who actually ended up with the hair they wanted, while the rest of us are all gnashing our teeth being straight desperate for curly, curly desperate for straight, or frizzy desperate for anything else.

"I've decided to grow my hair long," I told the Ginger when I got home, sporting Brown Bob No. 54. "You know, sort of Shania Twain-ish."

"Good," he said, his number-four clip ($7.50) glowing in the dim winter light. "I never liked Meg Ryan anyway."

PMT

CALL IT PMS, call it PMT, call it PM-bloody-ABC for all I care. Whatever it is, who needs it? After quarter of a century of having it foisted upon me at regular intervals, I woke up this morning knowing exactly what I want to do about it.

I want to find the half-baked, cretinous worm who came up with the concept and wring his neck with my bare hands.

Then I want to jump up and down on him. Then pull out his adenoids through his nose and make him eat them. Then kill him.

Then bring him back to life and make him listen to old Nana Mouskouri albums for 48 hours in a row with only Baileys Irish Cream for sustenance. Then kill him again.

It must have been a man, mustn't it?

God would still be feeling too sorry for us over the discrimination in the workplace thing to give us PMT, wouldn't he?

That and landing us with a monthly cycle — but at least the monthly cycle has a purpose.

Oh, and if any of you advertising whizzes out there are reading this, the purpose is not, by the way, to clog up our TVs with your meaningless drivel and ridiculously unbelievable scenarios involving great big dogs trying to get through tiny little holes to make us shop differently.

We'll just get what's cheapest in the supermarket, thank you.

And, in our spare time, we will bear your children for you, despite the fact we will probably all end up in the loony bin or at least surrounded by empty gin bottles when the little stinkpots come home from school saying they too want to be in advertising because the lunches are really long.

But at least our ovaries will have done their bit to fuel the planet's population.

PMT on the other hand — what does that contribute to the universe?

It contributes litres and litres of fluid from who knows where to places in your body (which, by the way, you despise) you have never even heard of.

It gets you more pimples than you had during the Peter Frampton years. It gives you bosoms so sore their natural force field repels all undergarments.

It gives you bad hair, dud clothes and a mean streak a mile wide.

It makes you loathe the colour ginger.

"Don't bring that thing near me," you shriek in a voice which strips the wallpaper.

"What thing, Sarah-Kate, who is pretty and sweet?" a voice stutters from underneath a pile of your shoes, all of which you hate and were recently airborne.

"That big round thing with all the ginger on top," you snarl, foaming at the mouth.

"That would be my head," the voice whispers.

"I don't care what you call it — get rid of it," you sob uncontrollably as you shovel a combination of four different sorts of ice-cream and a pizza into your mouth.

"And paint the house while you're at it," you weep, rubbing mozzarella across your tear-stained face.

"The colour is making me sad. No, happy. No, it's making me drop things. No, it reminds me of the babies in Ethiopia. Those poor little, brown babies."

You'll stop then. There's a light at the end of the tunnel.

You can make it through this. Everything will be okay. You just need chocolate.

Summer

SUMMER. HMM. On one hand, a fabulous season full of health and happiness, fun and sunshine. On the other, a time of deep gloom and depression induced by the cold, bleak prospect of shedding one's winter clothes.

You have probably guessed already I have just had THAT moment.

You know, the one when you slip into your togs for the first time, catch sight of yourself in the ranchslider and either gasp with shock or slip quietly into a coma.

Why, oh why didn't I start going to the gym in September like I said I would? Why did I not make cottage cheese my friend? Why did I think swaddling myself in an extra layer of chunky black was better than taking the stairs instead of the elevator?

The answer to these and other ridiculously reappearing questions cannot be found anywhere inside my head because I have looked.

So there I was again, staring down at an undulating expanse of lily-white thigh and gurgling with horror.

"What's the word for something spongy and white and hairy?" I asked the Ginger.

"Fatsquatch," he answered before the *Oxford Concise* hit him in the back of the head.

"Lamington!" my friend Jacque suggested before I decided she was too thin for me to talk to.

How could it be, I wondered, that my special paunch-sucking-in togs imported via the Internet from the US didn't make me look like a supermodel?

"A super model of what?" the Ginger asked dangerously when he regained consciousness. Goodness me but responding to vital signs can be over-rated. However, he had a point.

I did, in fact, look like a super model of something quite, sort of, well-built, fitted into something also quite, sort of, well-built but perhaps a bit smaller.

That's right, the special Spandex slender suit can do a lot of things but performing miracles isn't one of them. That paunch just has to go somewhere.

Nasa may have invented a swimming tog fabric which lets you sit on the barbecue plate for hours at a time without scorching but they've yet to come up with a solution for overflow — if you know what I mean.

Still, once I got over the disappointment of realising, yet again, the good elves hadn't secretly made me thin under my winter clothes, I remembered there are far worse things than overfilling your bathers.

Being arrested at the local mall for instance. Have you noticed how small children take fright and run screaming from absolutely nothing these days?

Really, all I did was elbow a handful of the little poppets out of the way, although perhaps from a distance it did look more like flinging and stomping.

What can I say? I had to get to the grotto in a hurry because the past few years Santa has gotten wind of my pending arrival and scarpered up the fire escape.

This year, I didn't want the old trickster to see me coming.

"It's your own stupid fault," I sobbed into his beard before the security guards came and dragged me away. "If you had given me muscly thighs and a flat stomach, like I asked for last Christmas, I wouldn't HAVE to sit on you again."

Legs

ONCE THE SUN finally came out and I could stop whingeing about the lack of hot weather, I suddenly remembered my legs are no longer fit for public consumption.

It's an age thing. Like going grey, liking *Coronation Street* and obsessing about bowel motions — it just creeps up on you.

One year, you are gallivanting around in cut-offs and, the next, you are standing in front of a shop window drooling as your reflection shouts, "For God's sake, woman, cover up."

Suddenly, you don't feel so crash-hot in your shorts any more. Suddenly, you're eyeing up wheelchairs and fantasising about getting your legs amputated in a horrible knitting accident.

Call me vain — or, more accurately, vein — but 38-year-old knees are just not an attractive sight.

There's something about them which reminds me of photos of myself $37\frac{1}{2}$ years ago and, frankly, it is not a look I was heading for. Although if I get desperate enough, I'm not beyond wearing smocks and matching bloomers, believe me.

These days, I will get my legs out but quite a few things have to fall into place first. Cover of darkness and everybody else being extremely drunk helps — a lot.

But unfortunately neither of these things usually happen at the same time as hot temperatures. (I'm working on this — with the help of global warming — but there are only so many aerosol sprays a girl can use at one time.)

If there are no very drunk people available, then no people at all will do but, even then, I have to avoid sitting down in my shorts and I have Elle Macpherson to thank for that.

When I was interviewing her a couple of years ago, she flashed me her knickers while in a seated position. It was a lingerie thing.

Until then, I had assumed everybody's thighs at least doubled in size when they sat down because of that evil spreading thing which happens.

But I can reveal here and now that Elle Macpherson's thighs

did not spread. They stayed the same size — and shape. There was no cellulite. She ate chocolates. Knife. Where is it? Stab.

Oh, where was I? My conditions? Yes, waxing must have taken place within recent weeks — if not minutes.

I don't know about you but I think the warm, wet weather has fertilised my leg hair because my pelt is taking off at an alarming rate. There's even a rumour going around the beauty parlour my waxer is retiring to a fully furnished condo on the Gold Coast on the proceeds of my leg hair removal fee alone.

Still, when everything comes together, it's worth it. There's nothing quite like the feeling of the cool breeze whistling around your pins — as long as you have the right footwear on of course.

My friend Kate's mother warned us some years ago that girls who wear clompy shoes never get husbands yet, despite this, I insist on having nothing but clomp in my closet.

To me, a serious piece of foot gear at the bottom of a leg somehow balances the non-Elle-like proportions of the upper leg, thereby reducing the "ice-cream cone effect" podgy thighs and slim-ish ankles can create.

Fear of the "ice-cream cone effect" is known by psychologists around the world to be a sign you are "completely barking mad" and probably don't have "anything better to worry about".

Still, if I can reduce that fear, get rid of the light, drink heavily, make sure Elle Macpherson isn't in the room and wax every half hour, I'll be quids in on the shorts front — and that's what counts.

Diets

ALTHOUGH I HAVE written a whole book about the silliness of dieting and how the wretched things never work, my Catholic guilt propels me to confess I'm once again on one.

You'll be pleased to know, however, that it's not working very well. So the book is right. So if it wasn't already out of print because people were too busy buying the liver cleansing book, you could feel quite justified in getting a copy.

Anyway, the diet I am on is not the normal sort, by which I mean I started this one nine months in advance of the event I want to be in good shape for, rather than nine hours. It makes all the difference, I tell you.

One day last year I instructed the Ginger in a cool and calm fashion that I wanted to be a comfortable size 16 by my 40th birthday, even if it was just for a day, and that from now on all my meals should reflect this endeavour.

I then had to spend a week explaining to him that despite me telling him for years that brown food has no calories, pies, chips and chocolate wouldn't, in fact, help me in my quest for shopping off the rack.

And once I drew a diagram with very complicated mathematical equations demonstrating exactly how diets work, he caught on big time. In fact he seemed mildly excited by the whole idea.

So the next few weeks were spent going about our business in the usual fashion with a healthy breakfast taken at the beginning of the day, followed by a medium sized lunch and rounded off with an alarmingly small dinner.

Naturally, I cheated. Not hugely but the odd glass or five of wine here and there. A pick-me-up bagel in the mid-afternoon on occasion, crackers and cheese at a friend's place of an evening. Well, it's rude not to. And anyway, that's how diets work.

Here's the thing though. That conniving former sponge known as the Ginger did not cheat. Apparently there is "no point" in cheating. Instead he just stuck to what he said he was going to stick to and lost 10kg. On MY diet. The cheek (much diminished) of him.

"You look so thin!" people started telling him. "You look so young!"

A smug little smile would trip across his lips before he would feel the cold, dark rumble of my baleful glare thundering towards him and immediately stick out the pathetic remains of his once undulating belly.

"What about Sarah-Kate?" he would say helpfully. "She's lost 5 kilograms."

His admirers would turn to me with stuck-on smiles and wide eyes.

"Ha ha. Yes. Glowing with health. Ahem."

"Tell her the thing about looking younger," the Ginger would encourage. "She likes that."

It all came to a rather horrible head when we went out to a fancy restaurant for dinner and the Ginger ordered potato mash but then wouldn't eat it because it tasted too creamy and buttery. I mean, hell-o-o-o-o-o.

If we were going to make it to May without one of us, I explained, namely him, being chopped up into tiny pieces and fed to the pigs, we had to reach an agreement.

And so, for the remaining months, when he is with me, the Ginger is required to share my diet to keep me on the straight and narrow. But when he is on his own he is required to eat lots of takeaways to keep himself less straight and narrow.

I don't think it's exactly helping him with the whole concept of dieting — but then it's a stupid concept anyway.

Good On Ya, Sport

Exercise

THE OTHER MORNING I was out jogging by the ocean, my sleek brown ponytail swishing across my back, when I looked down at my slim brown legs pounding the pavement and felt a rush of sheer pleasure.

"God, I love this," I shouted to the coconut palms, running my hands across my six-pack of abdominal muscles, exposed by way of my tight-fitting midriff top (which was totally free of perspiration, despite the rigour of the run).

"Oh, look — I'm Cindy Crawford," I marvelled.

Then I woke up.

I was lying in bed wearing two slightly soiled T-shirts, an old pair of the Ginger's boxer shorts and mismatched socks. My legs were not slim and brown. My hair was not sleek. My abdominal muscles were not available just then.

"Okay, I gotta get me some exercise," I decided, removing a piece of pizza from the side of my head.

Fighting the natural urge to finish the latest John Grisham offering, I staggered out of bed and fell on to the floor, where I did three sit-ups. Exhausted, I rolled over to continue my new regime with a clutch of press-ups but no matter how much I shouted "Give me 20", I seemed to remain dead-still in a heap on the floor.

My brain was having trouble working out which bits of me it had to send messages to, in order to lift me up and down. Instead, it was diverting its attention to Vegemite on toast, which it would normally be telling me to gobble down about now. Ignoring my brain — well, men do it all the time, don't they? — I crawled over to my wardrobe and tried to work out what Cindy would wear if she was me. I'm sure, if she actually was me, she would probably cover up a little bit more of herself than if she was just she.

We decided on adding tracksuit pants and a baggy sweatshirt to my existing ensemble. Then Cindy abandoned me while I tried to clean up my trainers, which were housing four different kinds of mould and three types of toadstools.

Eventually, I was ready for it — my first morning run.

Out the door I purposefully strode, breaking into a trot as I went. By the time I reached the letter box, I was gasping for breath. By the end of the road, I had thrown up twice and was crying.

Luckily, a neighbour took pity on me and drove me home, where I could rest, hyperventilating for a while.

That's when I remembered exercise and I don't mix.

How could I have forgotten? I've already tried swimming, cycling, skiing, horse-riding, basketball, jazzercise, step aerobics, pump classes, golf, tennis and tai chi and none of them took.

Aquarobics gave me the giggles, volleyball made me jiggle too much and a stint at home with a hired treadmill left the dog in therapy for months.

Team sports were out of the question because of the nuns and the whole hideous netball thing and that only left...

Well, what did it leave? I silently asked Cindy to send me a sign — please.

From under the stairs came the sound of a canine gently breaking wind. Of course. There it was, right under my nose — literally.

I might never have Cindy's long legs and washboard abs but a gentle walk with a farty pooch? Even I can handle that.

Skiing

THE NEXT TIME I show any sort of excitement about a skiing holiday, somebody please chop off my arms and legs and give me a good excuse to stay at home.

Yes, I know, I know — thousands of poor unfortunates lie awake at night and dream about being taken to the top of a snowy mountain and forced down the side of it. But the grass is always greener where there actually is some grass, if you ask me.

It's a complexion thing.

You see, my idea of the perfect holiday is scorching myself in a tropical climate, where piña coladas run wild and free — but, as I have mentioned in the past, I possess a husband of the ginger variety.

Put the poor creature in the harsh sunlight for more than five minutes and it's saveloys all round.

His idea of fun is being bundled up to avoid freezing his extremities off and whizzing down a mountain at high speed, strapped to slippery emery boards.

The being bundled up bit I don't mind. In fact, the skifield is one of the few places where thin people can't show off, because everybody's dressed up in variations on the lumpy theme. That, I like. The part where you point downhill and "go hard", I don't.

Amazingly, though, every year the Ginger organises a ski trip, I fail to fake a coma.

This is because I have a brain the size of a scorched almond and, every time I hear "skiing holiday", I skip happily over the skiing bit and concentrate solely on the holiday bit — knowing holidaying is something at which I excel, forgetting skiing is something at which I do the opposite.

So I get all excited and agree to go.

All through the planning stages I remain happily enthusiastic. As we drive hours through the winter wonderland of the South Island, I maintain my excitement. As we dress in chunky waterproofs and ugly hats, I dream of shooshing down the slopes.

But, as we arrive at the top of the snowy mountain, I have to go to the bathroom — three times. It's cold and wet and my feet hurt. "What the hell kind of holiday is this?" I snarl at the bewildered Ginger, as he drags me from the Ladies. "Where's the pool? Bring me my cocktail!"

About an hour later, you'll find me clinging to the side of the hill, sobbing as the people I've crushed while trying to get off the chairlift use what fingers they still have attached to their hands to dial their lawyers.

"It's just not enough fun," I sniff sadly, as a three-year-old skis past me at speed with a pitying look. Who knew you could suck on a dummy and look contemptuous at the same time?

Naturally, the Ginger's long gone by now. If the punch up after the chairlift pile-up wasn't enough, the avalanche of insults aimed at his parentage were. And that was before anyone else had a go at him.

No, it's up to me to get off this mountain on my own and, if I have to do it on my backside, well, another good use for a backside.

Besides, I thought I detected pie crumbs on the three-year-old. There must be pies down this here hill.

Pies, I can do.

Fishing

AS PART OF MY lifelong mission to find a sport at which I excel — other than smorgasbording, that is — I had the opportunity, recently, to try my hand at fishing.

Theoretically, fishing contains many of the elements I find essential in an activity. You don't wear skimpy clothes, you sit down a lot and, at the end of it all, you get to eat something.

This puts it well ahead of most other athletic pursuits as far as I'm concerned, so, when friends invited myself and the Ginger to spend a weekend at Lake Taupo, I was quick to accept. You know how I love a holiday.

The first day, the lake was too choppy, so we had to give boating a miss — for which I was grateful, as I hadn't really thought the fishing thing through too well.

Who knew there would be boating?

Boating doesn't fit my sporting criteria at all, because it involves an activity I avoid like the plague — having to climb in or out of things. An old friend of mine is still in hospital after attempting to load me on to a jet ski one summer in the 1970s.

I had imagined my fishing would take place at the end of a quaint little jetty, next to a picnic hamper, with perhaps a cappuccino stand nearby. You can imagine my surprise, then, when I was woken up at 6am by our spirited host singing the praises of the glassy lake and seemingly unaware the temperature was hovering around zero degrees.

Too stunned to argue, I staggered out of bed and pulled on 14 layers of clothes. I was still chilled to the bone, so I added a baseball cap, a balaclava and two pairs of socks, which I wore as mittens.

We drove to the boat ramp and unloaded our vessel — although I slept through this, huddled in the front seat with the heater on full and a few layers of the *Taupo Times* thrown over me for warmth.

When I woke up to the sound of the Ginger banging on the

window, I remembered I'd vowed never to return to Taupo, after being tricked by the local harbourmaster as a junior reporter into writing a story about a fancy new duckweed-eating barge called Donald.

Shaken by this memory, I stepped gingerly aboard our vessel from a jetty, conspicuous in its lack of quaintness, and the fishing commenced.

The highlight of the first hour was someone breaking open the bacon sarnies. Fantastic.

The highlight of the second, third and fourth hours was everyone catching a fish, if not two. Except me, that is, and I was hogging the "lucky" rod like there was no tomorrow.

"Once more around the lake," I cried, as I slung my hook for somewhere near the 99th time. "I too want to catch one of those shimmering beauties and bash its little head in with the spanner."

But the rainbow trout gods, just like the netball, skiing, tennis, windsurfing and golf gods, refused to smile on me.

The general consensus from my fishing buddies was that I'm a very good steerer.

It's not much, I know, but, at this stage in my sporting career I'll take what I can get.

The Olympics

IS IT JUST ME or are Olympic sports getting more and more loony?

As you may have picked up, I'm not very sporty but I'm no slouch when it comes to the remote control so I do take a passing interest in major events such as the Olympics.

Track and field I can understand. Swimming? Of course. Equestrian? Well, we're good at that so why not?

But beach volleyball? Give me a break.

One can only imagine Pamela Anderson was sitting in on the Olympic committee the day they okayed that baby. What's next? Gold medals (two of course) for the best wet T-shirt wearer?

If the beach volleyballers were made to wear old St Mary's cast-off regulation bloomers and three layers of jumpers designed to foil any chance of spotting a nipple, one has to wonder if the sport would have squeaked on to the world stage quite so easily.

Mind you, the Catholic Olympics would be a whole different event all together.

No skimpy outfits. No contact sports. No getting too big for your boots. No showing your knickers at the pole vault. No four-letter words when the next guy does better. All medals to be shared with those less fortunate than yourself.

On the plus side, banned substances wouldn't get a look in. Who's going to toy with cocaine when chewing gum in public is punishable by death?

A quick call to an athlete's parents would put a stop to most questionable behaviour and, if it didn't — well, nobody wants to stay behind after the Games to help tidy up now, do they?

On the subject of banned substances, a friend of mine and I were considering this in great detail over a gin and tonic, or seven, the other day.

We'd already spent half an hour on the difficulty of finding a good dental floss and felt we had to move on to something more substantial.

Having both been schooled by nuns, we're obviously sadly lacking any personal experience in the field of banned substances but watch a lot of Hollywood movies, closing our eyes for the sex scenes but opening them when people stick things up their noses.

How exactly, my friend wanted to know, did cocaine enhance a sporting performance anyway?

"Unless it's the 'Talking A Lot Very Quickly' Olympics, in which case people like us would be gold medallists without the slightest bit of help," he said, taking another slurp.

Frankly I think the people who dream up the sports are the ones on drugs.

Handball? Puh-leeze. Those crazy Swedes! One minute, they're working out how to round off the small change at the supermarket and the next they are reigning world handball champions.

I've yet to watch a game but what's the bet there are very small bits of Spandex and a lot of jumping around involved?

What I look forward to most during the Games is watching the rhythmic gymnastics. This is when all the little pint-sized Gumby-girls-of-clay run around the floor with a hoop or some clubs or a big long ribbon.

It's sort of like the juggling Olympics but without size 64 shoes and a red plastic nose. Sadly men are not allowed to enter this event, nor can they join a synchronised swimming team.

Such a shame. I'm sure an All Black-like team in butt-thongs and nose clips wearing hats like hydrangea flowers would give those Aussies a run for their money.

That'd have to help even the score.

Tramping

MEN, WHEN THEY hit a certain age, tend to celebrate by swapping their wives for a stick figure fresh from the local high school and buying a Harley Davidson so they can wear leather without seeming creepy. About which, might I add, they are wrong.

Women, on the other hand, in their EXTREMELY late, in fact as late as you can possibly get, thirties, often break out of their moulds but in different, less laughably pathetic, ways.

For some it's swapping looking after the kids for getting a job, for others it's swapping a stink job for another stink job — but with better hours — and for others it is conquering new and exciting challenges about the likes of which they have barely bothered to dream in the past.

Since I don't have kids or a job but am in the right age bracket, it is to the latter I have found myself drawn and in a fit of feeling the fear and doing it anyway, I have agreed to, gulp, go tramping.

If you are not laughing by now, can I tell you that you are in a group of just one person.

I don't know why the idea of myself laden with dehydrated food stuffs, billies, bunsen burners and tent pegs is so blooming hilarious. I have legs, haven't I? Walking shouldn't be something that it is unlikely for me to do a lot of.

"Oh, Gawd," was all the Ginger could say when I told him I had booked to walk the Routeburn Track with a friend while he stayed behind in Queenstown and worked. "Who will carry your pack?"

He had me there. I hadn't thought of that.

"Oh, it's not that sort of tramp," I said airily.

But upon reading the fine print in the brochure, I discovered it was that sort of tramp. It would appear that all tramps, even ones where you get to sleep in a bed and have wine with your three-course meals, involve carrying a pack.

"You get to sleep in a bed and have wine with your three-course meals?" asked another very unsupportive friend when she finished wiping the tears of laughter from her eyes.

"Why don't you just get a helicopter to just chopper you from lodge to lodge?" (I checked. They don't do that.)

Determined to prove all my oh-so-hilarious friends wrong, I went straight into training. That is, I bought a lovely pair of tramping boots.

"Oh, Gawd," the Ginger said when he saw them sitting at the back door.

"Shouldn't you be wearing them in?" he asked nervously a couple of days later. "Or, at least, just wearing them?"

"Are you on drugs?" I trilled. "They'll get dirty!"

At this point he sat me down and gave me a little chat about tramping.

"You will have to carry your own clothes and toiletries," he warned. "It may not be very warm. It may rain a lot. You might get muddy. Your feet, you know, the things that get blisters from looking at a pair of jandals? They may be rubbed raw and make each step an exercise in spine-tingling pain. You will be walking up to seven hours a day so you will be stiff and sore from the day before. I will not be there to rub your back and dry your clothes and get a second helping of pudding which I will pretend is for me but which is really for you."

"I've already paid," I said.

"You'll love it," he answered.

The Routeburn Track

DESPITE EXTENSIVE training for my first tramping experience, I woke up on the morning of my departure for the Routeburn Track guided walk hoping that small furry animals had nibbled off my extremities in my sleep.

Sadly all body parts were present and accounted for and it was too early to think of another excuse to stay at home so off into the wilderness I toddled.

The first few hours were spent in a bus en route to the drop-off point round Milford way. This was most picturesque, not to mention nice and dry, but to give you a really accurate impression of just how much I am NOT a tramper, I got a blister on my heel during this part of the journey. That's right. Sitting in an air-conditioned bus seat looking out a window. Go figure.

Anyway, we eventually staggered out of the bus and attached our packs then walked for an hour or so uphill until we came to the top of a mountain surrounded by more scenery than you could poke a stick at. The sun was shining, the peaks were snow-capped and the view was glorious. Suddenly I could see what this tramping business was all about.

From up there too, we could look across and spot, at similar height a few mountains away, the valley where we'd be staying the night. No problems there, I thought.

Until we started to go downhill again.

But why, I wanted to know, would we want to go downhill when we had only just gone uphill and would clearly have to be going uphill again? Wasn't that a waste of going uphill in the first place? The "because it's there" mentality, it turns out, has totally escaped me.

Lunch, of course, cheered me up enormously especially as it came with chocolate, which apparently has no calories when eaten at high altitudes. My feet, however, were giving me gyp. I had no feeling whatsoever in my left toes and a shooting pain across the top of my right foot. I was having trouble not moaning. And this was the beginning of the first day.

Luckily, there was technical advice at hand in the form of a very experienced scientist and wilderness equipment handler. "Loosen your laces," he suggested, which solved all my problems. Ahem.

By five I had staggered up (and down and up again) to our accommodation for the night. There was a fire roaring and cheese and biscuits on the table and I thought I had died and gone to heaven.

Also, I had just bumped into a girl I babysat 25 years ago, which proved to the group I was hiking with that everyone in New Zealand does actually know each other, and that was nice, don't you think?

Day two was a lot like day one only with low visibility, a chill wind and some dampness. A lot of uphill was followed by some lovely downhill then we had steak for dinner and wine — out of a cask but wine nonetheless.

Day three was more like day two, only wetter, but by then I was a bona fide mountain woman. I had had the same long johns on for three days and my boots were no longer shiny and new.

My hair looked like something you find squashed on the side of a country road and I smelled quite strongly of wet woolly jumpers.

But by 2pm I was skipping down the last bit of the track splashing in puddles and shouting, "I walked the Routeburn! I walked the Routeburn!"

I'm right outdoorsy, me.

Wrinkles and Rankles

Ageing

FOR A WHILE NOW, I've been fighting an unexplained urge to run over young women with bouncy ponytails and strappy tops.

At first, I thought it was something my car was doing which was completely out of my control. (Like the time I took it to the mechanic, because it was making clunking noises when it went around corners only to find out the problem could be traced immediately to seven half-empty plastic drink bottles careering around the boot.)

But recently, as I scrutinised the shiny locks, skinny arms and wrinkle-free faces which were irritating me so, I realised with horror why I wanted their presence removed.

These girls are very young.

I am not.

I've never been the jealous type before but, then again, I've never been a grey-haired, cranky old wrinkly in a sea of nubile young wenches before, either.

When did young women start wearing so little? I tell you, there ought to be a law.

If they are going to flaunt their tight underarms and uncrepey skin and all that shiny hair which has never seen a dye bottle, then surely they deserve to be thrown to the ground and trampled.

Why aren't their mothers locking them up in dark closets to stop their youthfulness from upsetting us old crumblies anyway? We have rights, you know.

How can I be expected to keep clinging to the life raft of my youth when these hipster-wearing midriff barers are stomping on my fingers? It's a disgrace.

The thing is, I'm just not ready for middle age, despite the fact I now seriously want to know what is going to happen next on *Coronation Street* and honestly can't understand why modern youth listen to such drivel on their record players.

Luckily for me, though, I happened to be at home one day

recently when Oprah did a show on how to be younger than you actually are.

Unfortunately, I missed out on quite a few details, because the phone kept ringing and, as I pretend I never watch daytime telly, I had to keep turning the sound down.

The gist is, if you do a few simple things often enough, you slow down the ageing process and your "real" age becomes much younger than your "biological" age.

For example, a French woman whose biological age was 52 had a real age of 36.8 because she did 90 minutes a day of Latin American dancing and bonked a lot.

Actually, it may have been banking she did a lot of — but I was lipreading at the time, so can't be sure.

Anyway, things which can definitely take years off you are wearing sunglasses, having friends (worth a fabulous 30 years!), bathing not more than once a day and doing stomach crunches.

Also, according to Oprah's experts, eating chocolate before dinner is anti-ageing, and, get this, wine makes you younger. I know that's true, because Oprah did a little jig and sang a song about how great that was.

So I've employed some of these helpful hints and worked out my real age — which as it happens is 12, although there's a chance I may have confused Oprah's calculation with the formula for converting Fahrenheit into Celsius.

But, this way, at least the strappy, bouncy women of the world are again safe to walk the streets.

Facials

EVEN AT MY ADVANCED age I'm something of a newcomer to make-up and have yet to really get a grip on it.

Lipstick, I understand. I may have thin lips but one of the great benefits (okay, the only benefit) is being able to apply lipstick without looking in a mirror. Oh, how the full-lipped girls look on in admiration!

Mascara, yes. On the plus side it gives you bigger lashes. On the minus side, though, you might forget you are wearing it and rub your orbs thereby ending up looking like a thin-lipped panda.

Everything in between, I'm a little hazy on. Sure I have a purse full of foundation and eye shadow and blusher in the finest shade of terracotta but it spends a lot more time heating up in the car than being applied to my face.

Well, the rest of my body might be approaching 39 but I've always believed the skin on my face remains that of a youthful princess.

You can imagine my surprise, then, when I received a facial voucher inside a "Happy 40th Birthday!" card from a friend — and I use the term loosely — in the mail.

"You never liked her anyway," the Ginger reminded me as I hyperventilated at the letter box. "You always said she could never, um, count. Oooh, and she has thick ankles. Remember?"

Once I stopped trying to work out if being mistaken for 40 was worse than being considered in need of substantial wrinkle work, I decided not to look a gift cow in the mouth and booked in for the facial. What the hey. Getting old is expensive. You take the freebies where you can.

The moment I walked into the beauty parlour though, I started to panic. It smelled like camomile tea bags and there was the sound of waves crashing and, if I'm not mistaken, dolphins calling to each other. I felt like someone's crazy-haired cousin from the sticks turnin' up for what you fancy city folks call pamperin' and not liking it. Not one iota. Suddenly I understood the term "out of your comfort zone". If my actual comfort zone was, say, a small settlement just out of Hamilton, I was in Whangarei.

We walked up a corridor arriving at a room in Cape Reinga where I was asked to take my top off and lie down on the bed.

"If I wake up implanted with an alien embryo," I thought to myself, "I am going to KILL the bad-counting, off-the-Christmas-card-list, never-to-be-spoken-to-again B-I-T-C-H who got me into this."

Minutes later, my technician was asking me in soothing tones about my beauty routine. "Well, I wash my face with water," I said, "and for the past two years I have been using a moisturiser. Every day!"

I heard a sharp intake of breath.

"Oh no," she said, shaking her head. "You really MUST use a cleanser and a toner. You really must. You need to rid your skin of all its impurities. The pollution! The oil! The ravages of a normal day in the city at your age.

"What I'm going to do is apply this mask made from seaweed and algae and…"

It was too much. I drifted off.

When I awoke, however, there was no alien life form squirming inside me. Just the hazy memory of creamy lotions, warm flannels, calming gels, crashing waves, camomile tea and dolphins.

"I'll take a cleanser and one of them tonics," I said, once firmly back in my comfort zone. Which, as it happened, turned out to be the shop in the front.

"And a little thank you gift for the dear friend who sent me here."

Parties

AFTER A COUPLE of decades of not getting invited to any parties at all, I find myself once again on this most exhausting of social circuits. I must have been to four already this year.

No wonder my eyes have bags under them and I need extra moisturising.

The thing is, wherever I turn, my friends are turning 40, poor things, and these days, the pressure's on to fork out for a bit of a shindig to commemorate this milestone.

The last time I suffered such a rash of partying was for their 21sts and, frankly, I'm still recovering from some of those.

Actually, as a younger person, I never much fancied parties. They all seemed full of people shorter, thinner, better dressed and more fabulous than myself. Two from my late teens do stick out though.

One was an "S" party we hosted in our first Wellington flat in the days when you could fill a flagon of wine for four bucks. Hey, the headache was worth it.

It's the only fancy dress party I've ever been to where everybody played the game and we had everything from Sisters of Mercy, to skeletons, to four girls in white shirts spelling out S-H-I-T.

The only slight downer was that, as the night went on, the scarecrow got progressively unstuffed by a subdural haematoma and, no matter how much we vacuumed, we never quite got all the straw.

Another time, a flatmate who worked at the theatre got us three penguin suits which we wore to a fellow student's fancy dress party — only to discover that all the other girls had gone as saucy saloon girls or movie stars.

While they sashayed their way flirtatiously around the blokes, we were forced against the wall, sweating like hogs, unable to eat or drink or even smoke fags owing to the fact penguins have wings, not hands.

Plus we couldn't find a taxi to take us home so we had to waddle. Where is the World Wildlife Foundation when you need it, eh? All these years later, I have discovered the good thing about 40th birthdays is that either people have got taller, fatter, worse dressed and less fabulous or I've stopped noticing as much — because the parties I've been to so far this year have been a blast. And one of them even started at 7.30pm and everybody was there on time. How we would have laughed 19 years ago!

So there is a lot more talk about baby-sitters and mortgages and nowhere near as much snogging as there used to be (guess I have to wait for the 50ths for that) but, these days, you get a sit-down meal with your party and that can't be bad.

The last one I went to, we even pushed back the tables and danced to our favourite tunes from the 1980s, getting home at 2.30am, hoarse from singing and limping from a hip creak brought on by excessive gyrating to the Pretenders.

"At my 40th," I said to the Ginger the next morning, "there's going to be a DJ playing all my favourite disco hits."

"So, you're having a 40th now are you?" purred the Ginger, smug in a way only a 36-year-old can be.

"Yes," I said.

"Although it is many, many, many, many, many weeks away, I have decided one thing."

"Oh yes?"

"You're not invited."

Sure, he can help with the catering but he's too young to appreciate the rest.

Bars

SO THERE I WAS with Dangerous Cousin Dave and the Ginger standing in a bar, chewing the fat. It was late. We'd had a couple of drinks before dinner, then hit the strip, up on Auckland's Ponsonby Road.

Some fashionable types at the restaurant had pointed us in the direction of a new drinking emporium which they claimed was the current hot spot. Turns out it was an old drinking emporium which had been a former hot spot, only now it had orange chairs. It was dark, there were good-looking guys on the door, the night was young. We were three hip, crazy, country cats in town for a big night out and we were going to stop at nothing.

"Yeez," I said to Dangerous Cousin Dave. "Seven bucks fifty for a poxy glass of wine?"

"What?" he mouthed over the din.

"I said the drinks cost heaps," I shouted over the oonst, oonst, oonst of the bass beat.

"It does a bit," he answered. "I think the carpet must be damp."

"No," I shouted, "I said they sting you on the tipple!"

"Well, ping them right back," he roared, looking slightly disgusted.

"What did he say?" the Ginger wanted to know.

"Something about slingbacks," I sighed. "Can we go now?"

He looked at me doubtfully. "I don't know if it's a hoedown sort of a place."

It was then I experienced a moment of dark and deep-rooted depression. The drinks were too expensive, it was smoky, it was dark, the music was too loud, I couldn't hear a word anybody said and all the other girls didn't have enough clothes on. In other words, I was old.

What made this all seem worse was that I was being old in the very same spot I had been young in many, many, many times before, pre-orange chairs.

What had happened to me that I could no longer spend hour

after hour perched on a barstool shouting utter bollocks to whoever had the misfortune to be on either side of me?

Some of my best memories are of being in smoky bars late at night clutching a chardonnay and having a chin wag.

Okay, so I don't smoke any more but I'm no stranger to a dry white wine and my chin wags more than ever.

Outside on the street, we talked to each other in low voices just to celebrate the fact that it was possible.

"I'm sorry but I like to be able to hear what people say," Dangerous Cousin Dave said. "Yeez. Maybe I'm old too."

We looked at the Ginger.

"Insert the correct response," he said, which I thought was quite clever.

Turns out the Ginger likes it much better now that I am old. It means the 4am phone calls asking him what my PIN number is are less frequent.

And Dangerous Cousin Dave, whose motto used to be "you don't need a plan to lean against a bar", has now had to change his motto to "Give us a Speights and shut up for a bit, would you."

So there we were, three hip, crazy, country cats in town for a big night out. It had just turned 11pm.

"I think I'll head off," said Formerly Dangerous Cousin Dave.

Seeing the disappointment on my face, the Ginger inserted the correct response. "I put the electric blanket on three before we came out," he whispered.

Old, schmold. "Taxi!"

Spots

THERE'S SOMETHING horribly wrong with the ageing process, in case you hadn't noticed. It seems to happen at a time when you least need it.

When you're young and thin, for example, you think you're fat and unattractive but you're not. Then, many years later, when you are actually fat and unattractive, it turns out you're old as well. Where's the love in that, I ask you?

I'm particularly bitter and twisted at the moment because I am sporting two particularly fetching spots on my dial — one the size of a large pea on the end of my nose and one the size of Palmerston North on my chin.

Now, it would seem to me that one of the benefits of being old and wrinkly and slightly saggy would be that you don't need to worry about acne any more.

Hah! That has not turned out to be the case.

In fact, I swear I get more great honkers these days than I ever did as a teenager and they seem to last forever and remain impenetrably un-squeezable.

"Step away from the mirror," the Ginger roared at me from under the duvet when I sneaked under cover of darkness into the bathroom for a good pick the other night. "Leave them alone."

Suddenly I heard the words of the nine-year-old girl who gave me a facial earlier in the year swimming around me, a chorus of dolphins in the background, "You really MUST use a cleanser and a toner. You really must!"

Maybe she had been on to something trying to force me to spend hundreds of dollars to unclog my pores with fancy potions. Maybe you can't just do it with hot shower water and a 12-year-old nailbrush.

"I think we may need to re-mortgage the house so that I can get rid of these festering sores," I told the Ginger the next morning. "I need to buy a lot of stuff that looks like poop but is in fact made of algae to put on my face to dry out the epidermal canals."

"I thought you told me pimples were God's way of showing you everything was still working?" he replied.

"That was when it was somebody else who had them," I replied. "In fact, I now realise that pimples are God's way of showing you crow's feet and underarm flab are not as bad as it gets."

At this, the Ginger flinched, looked terrified for a moment, then put on a kind fatherly face and patted me on the shoulder. (I taught him this after the "you're not as old as you look" episode of 1999.)

"Has it occurred to you," he said gently, "that perhaps your spots are not as obvious to everyone else as they are to you?"

"Honey," I replied, "the post man has names for them. He wants to know if they need their own address."

I saw the Ginger's eyes swivel around in his head as his brain attempted to alight on the right thing to say.

He had "don't mention you're not as old as you look" written all over him.

"In that case," he said, his orbs finally spinning to a halt as he hit on a winner, "has it occurred to you that that great huge Vesuvius on your chin might actually make you look younger than you really are?"

Undergarments

EVER SINCE I turned 40, a whole new world has opened up to me and I am truly loving it. Turns out there are some things worth getting older for.

One such thing has changed my life so much I can't believe my forty-something friends kept me in the dark for so long. But it would appear there's an unspoken agreement between women of a certain age not to mention certain things and this is one of them.

And here was I thinking that once you got into that new decade, things started to droop and sag and otherwise hit the floor. "Oh no you don't," my older (by two weeks) friend Ronnie counselled me when I complained to her about feeling lumpy in my party outfit. "Or at least, oh no you WON'T."

Before I could ask her what the hell she was on about, we were in the car driving at breakneck (exaggeration, officer) speed towards Smith & Caughey's in Auckland. Up the escalator we went and straight to the lingerie department — which was pretty impressive as Ronnie doesn't even live in Auckland — or New Zealand for that matter.

But there in the barren desert of tiny g-strings stood the golden oasis she had sniffed out while flying over the city hours before. Apparently, if you're 40, you can see them from space. The Nancy Ganz stands, that is, because it is Nancy Ganz of which I speak.

Nancy, whoever she is, has become the goddess of the Extreme Thirty set by inventing a series of undergarments known as body slimmers, which can transform a girl's curves unlike anything else — other than life-long, round-the-clock liposuction.

Now, I'm breaking the code here so if you are not yet 40, go immediately to the bathroom and flush your head down the toilet until you are.

If you are 40, sell your hair, rent out the kids, hock off your jewels, do whatever you can to get yourself into this gear.

"Aha!" Ronnie said, plucking off the rack a small black slip that looked like something Liz Hurley might loan Pamela Anderson for a night out on the tiles. "Nancy-neck-to-knee. My favourite. Try it on."

Oh how I laughed. "If you think I can get into THAT," I said, "you've been drinking."

"Sarah-Kate," she replied, "we just turned 40. Of course, we've been drinking. We may never stop. Now try it on."

In the changing rooms, the Nancy-neck-to-knee put up quite a struggle. At first I tried to get her over my head but that was too scary. Then I tried applying her from below. I got as far as my knees before her Lycra/Spandex/Elastane/Polyamide combination got me in its vice-like grip and refused to budge. It took another half-hour of shoving and heaving and pushing and pulling but suddenly Nancy popped into place and — voila!

I looked at myself in the mirror and — gasp! — I was Elle Macpherson. (I told you I'd been drinking.)

Okay, I may not have been Elle Macpherson but I was a size smaller inside Nancy than I was anywhere else in the world and I couldn't get to the counter and hand over a large box of cash quickly enough.

It's been three weeks since that day and Nancy-neck-to-knee and I have become practically inseparable. We would be literally inseparable had I not trained the Ginger to help me remove her.

And if you doubt my allegiance to this undergarment in any way, let me tell you, she requires handwashing.

That's right, handwashing. Such is my devotion. Why, it's a wonder the Ginger has time to go to work with all his new laundry duties.

In the House

Reality TV

WHO WOULD HAVE THOUGHT reality TV would be such a goer? I always thought the whole point of TV was to be unrealistic — that's why I liked it.

Me, I prefer to live in a world where hospital beds are filled by people who work in the clinic, high schools are only for thin blondes and Mafia men gone bad are riddled with bullets and killed stone dead, only to turn up in another show hours later looking 10 years younger. That's my kind of reality.

None of this being stuck on a desert island with a bunch of beefy idiots all making each other cry and showing off about who can solve clues the quickest. No sirree.

And as for poking a bunch of Aussies in the same room and watching them ablute for week after week in their natural habitat? I don't think so. Just watching the promos sends my eyelids fluttering towards my cheeks in quest of a snooze.

Anyway, it's not reality. If only getting rid of dud flatmates was as easy as putting it to the vote, eh? We've all been there. Why, I never would have lasted more than a few minutes had the vote system been implemented in my day.

My idea of reality would be to stick a batch of cameras in a house where people DIDN'T know they were being filmed. Picture that, eh?

Some great lump of a husband gets up in the morning, scratching his paunch and belching his dragon-breath about the place before heading to the lav for a cacophony of bowel movements — now that would be eye-catching.

His wife rolls her eyes and keeps snoring until the dog comes and licks her on the mouth. And it's not the first place his tongue has been that morning either, if you know what I'm saying.

The kids start making a racket in the kitchen.

Little Benji is making a fort out of some knickers Mum bought really cheap because the elastic was faulty, while his big sister is experimenting with smoking marjoram out of the herb rack.

There are mouldy things in the fridge and Dad's boots are in the microwave.

A large bottle of lice treatment is sitting with the salt and pepper on the kitchen table and the cat is on the bench eating what remains of last night's fish fingers and instant mashed potato.

What fun it would be, trying to find out who these slobs really were.

My own husband, of course, would never scratch his paunch first thing. His itchy spots occur lower on the anatomy. I never snore and our dog doesn't lick his private parts — they are impeccably clean already.

My knicker elastic is — actually, now I look at it, pretty tragic — but our fridge is... oh, when did that start growing? And as for fish fingers? Ahem. Very nutritional, I believe.

Well, now I understand why reality TV isn't really reality. Reality can be quite disgusting. Reality could put a viewer off his cheese toasties.

Suddenly, I see why girls in skimpy bikinis might be introduced to take the edge off. I suppose it makes sense to introduce an island or a spot of outback to improve the view.

And maybe cracking codes and finding treasure is more interesting to watch than going to work and doing the crossword in the loo.

Still, I'll probably stick to *Coronation Street*. It's as much reality as I can stand.

Computers

NEXT TO MY sewing machine, there is only one inanimate object (not counting the Ginger) which can drive me to physical violence — and that is my computer.

This is because I am one of a new breed of human, known as a Technosput.

Not scared of technology — oh no, far from it — we Technosputs embrace it closely and, indeed, rely on it completely and utterly, not only for our livelihood but just for getting from one day to the next without a hernia.

Our problem is, that should anything go wrong with any of this technology, we are not in a position to fix it. We are not even in a position to know the words to explain what has gone wrong.

"When I pressed the big button at the front, it just sort of went grey, then it got a bit greyer and then a little foldery-type thing with a question mark on it came up," I bleated down the phone to the computer-fixing man the other day.

"Did you blah blah (something complicated) the blah blah (something even more complicated) with the blah blah?" (I'd stopped listening at this point.)

"Yes," I lied. "And then everything went away."

"Okay. Bring it in," he said.

"Well, I would," I lied, "but someone's stolen the steering wheel out of my car and there are just too many corners between my place and yours.

"Isn't there just a special way of, like, whacking it or something that you could tell me about over the phone?"

Truth was, I didn't want him to know it was Julie Andrews who had crashed my computer. I like her but she's possibly not considered hip in techno-boffin circles.

Because my computer has a hole for CDs to go into, you see, I had put my *Sound of Music* soundtrack in there — but half way through *The Lonely Goatherd*, the whole thing went kaput.

When I realised the CD was Von-Trapped inside, I tried to

release it with a safety pin. Then the safety pin got stuck inside too.

I didn't really want the computer-fixing man to see all this so, instead, I spent an hour extracting very technical recuperative specifications from him.

Then, after I hung up and couldn't make head or tail of my notes, I turned the whole thing on and off at the wall a few dozen times and eventually the problem went away!

So the bluey-green beast was saved from being thrown out the window yet again.

Next day, however, I turned it on only to have everything in sight eaten up by a fast-moving snake of strange symbols. My *New Zealand Woman's Weekly* columns, book chapters, e-mail addresses, whatever document I opened, the snake chewed up the contents.

Julie Andrews had given the thing a virus. And she looks like such a nice girl.

"Step away from the computer," the Ginger shouted as I slapped at the thing using all the swearwords I knew to tell it how I was going to hurl it down a cliff face and dance on the spot it used to occupy.

Fuming in a separate room some time later, it occurred to me there was something strangely familiar about that snake of strange symbols.

Slipping underneath the Ginger's cordon, I snuck up close to the offending computer and examined the keyboard.

Ah ha! I had been right. The 8 key was stuck down. And while one 8 just looks like an 8, a lot of 8888888888888s look like a virus — to a Technosput anyway.

So Julie hadn't stiffed me after all. The relief!

Tradesmen

WHO CARES IF the sparky sticks his nose in your knickers when he comes to fiddle with your light switch, I say. At least he's turned up.

Many of us would gladly swap all our soiled lingerie — and throw in a batch of freshly baked scones and our first-born child to boot — if the pantysniffer would just turn up at the agreed time on the agreed day and, at some stage during behaving inappropriately, fix the blasted lights.

If he wants to flick through the CD collection, watch Oprah, sell the furniture, traumatise the cat and serve finger food for 15, fine. If he wants to rub himself up and down against your passport photo, laugh at your wedding video, deface your secret David Cassidy stash, erase your phone messages, okay. If he wants to charge you three times in Auckland what he would in Wellington, hey, even that's cool. After all, that's what Aucklanders are for.

Any of the above, all of the above are nothing — I say NOTHING — compared to the havoc which can be wreaked on your life by the electrician/plumber/locksmith/washing machine man failing to show up at all. Because despite the fact we can fly to the moon, e-mail Zanzibar and ring the Antarctic, we still have to take time off work to wait at home until the tradesman comes.

Yep, I bet that will really impress the scientists from the planet Ghrk when they come to Earth to complete an advanced study of our civilised society. "I'm terribly sorry, Mr President," their antennae will pick up. "I'd love to continue our talks about world peace. We were so close. But there's a terrible smell coming from my dishwasher and I have to dash home now because The Man is coming to fix it between 1pm and 5pm today, 2pm and 6pm tomorrow, 10am or 1pm next Wednesday and maybe the following 19 Fridays at 7am or 3pm after that."

"Zhrg mmmmmx aHjj?" the alien scientists will gasp.

(Translation: Does she mean THE president?) "Pfffftt urg nsh-qlk ahoooga?" they'll continue. (Translation: Why doesn't The Man just come at 1pm today to fix the dishwasher, so she can nip home in her lunch hour to let him in and then get on with her life?)

Oh those silly Ghrkins! Such an uncomplicated, simple species.

They'll never last long here on Earth. Hopefully, they'll go home before they try to get a phone line put in, because the frustration of that will drive them to septic tank addiction or — even worse on Ghrk — leave them dependent on middle-of-the-night talk-back radio, a crime punishable by death.

Recent attempts by myself to pay even more money to Telecom by adding another two phone lines were foiled by the fact Telecom, for some reason, couldn't ring to tell us exactly when The Man would come to put them in. Neither could it fax us, email us, call either of our two mobile phones or leave a message on our Call Minder service.

Someone must have been working very hard to not be able to do any of that.

Anyway, I'd better go because the sink is blocked and I have to get home in time to wear all my undergarments, make two dozen muffins and get Fluffy all psyched up in case the plumber comes.

Domestic Bliss

I'M PROBABLY NOT the wife most likely to be found in the kitchen wearing a pinny and whistling happy tunes while I rustle up a perfect pot roast. But I like the sound of that wife, so when it became clear that moving to Queenstown meant the Ginger would be working 12-hour days while I stayed at home being creative, I decided I would give being that wife a go.

Being creative, as it happened, just didn't take up enough time.

"You're going to cook AND clean?" the Ginger asked in a jittery fashion. "Oh boy."

"Well, how hard can it be?" I snapped. "You've been doing it for the past 12 years, after all."

He muttered something that sounded a lot like "My point exactly," but which he insisted wasn't. Then he went off to work leaving me with only a day to plan, shop for and cook an evening meal.

I spent the morning in bed reading *Happy Days with the Naked Chef*. I'd tried Nigella Lawson's book but found her way too good-looking and sexy, which put me in a bad mood, so I ripped her into tiny pieces and fed her down the waste disposal unit.

"What will I have for lunch?" I asked the Ginger when I rang him at midday. "All this research is making me hungry."

I have to confess, I'm probably not what you would call a natural in the kitchen. My idea of cooking involves a jar of Vegemite and two slices of bread and in this cold climate, I even have trouble with that — the bread is too holey or something.

Anyway, after the Ginger talked me through baked beans on toast, I set off to the supermarket with my shopping list. Once there, however, I struck a few problems. The lamb racks weren't French, the tomatoes weren't plum, the olive oil wasn't virgin enough and there was no basil or marjoram. Now I can follow a recipe just as well as the next person, but improvise? I bought three packets of Sultana Bran and went home.

We had takeaways that night.

Next day I attempted the supermarket again only to find that the chickens weren't free range, the peppers were nearly $9 a kilogram and there was basil and marjoram but no tarragon. Also, the man in front of me in the queue accidentally took my shopping bag, which meant that when I got home I had no diet tonic water or pretzels either.

We ate out that night.

The next day I swapped Jamie Oliver for *Baker* by Dean Brettschneider and Lauraine Jacobs and that night for our dinner I cooked the most delicious carrot cake all on my own using every implement in the house.

"No entrée?" the Ginger asked querulously. "No main?"

"Just plenty of dessert," I said enthusiastically, tucking into my second slice. Boy, that cream cheese icing sure gets to you after a while. Lying on the sofa some time later, clutching my sides and listening to my stomach perform experimental percussion pieces, I suddenly noticed how many cobwebs there were. And the dust in the air — why, I could barely see the TV. Eegad! I had been so busy not cooking, I had also not cleaned. This domestic bliss business, I suddenly realised, sucked.

In fact, the more I thought about it, the more I didn't want to BE the wife who wears the pinny and happily pots the roast. I wanted to HAVE that wife. I turned to look at the Ginger.

"Give a little whistle, would you?" I asked in my nicest voice.

The Big Wide World

Irish Roots

WELL, THERE WE WERE — the lovely ginger husband and myself hurtling around the windswept high roads and by-roads of County Cork in Ireland, searching for the last surviving member of my mother's maternal Emerald Isle ancestors.

Spookily, the windswept high roads and by-roads of County Cork looked hauntingly similar to the windswept high roads and by-roads of the Scottish Highlands, where only two years before we'd hurtled around, looking for any signs of my mother's paternal ancestors.

Late 19th-century Manawatu must have seemed positively exotic in comparison!

Anyway, back in Cork, we were on the trail of one Theresa Roberts, the niece of my great-grandmother. All we knew was she was in her nineties and lived with her cousins, Connie and Mary Lucey, in a place called Rathura.

Well, we might have known that but, sadly, the maps of the area were nowhere near as knowledgeable. Not a Rathura to be found in maps 1, 2 or 3 and only a tiny, little Ratooragh in map 4, so we headed for there.

"Ratooragh?" the woman behind the hardware store counter asked when we were still totally Ratooragh-less after many kilometres of highways and byways. "Sure, it's past Ahakista. Go there and ask at the pub."

"Ratooragh?" roared the barman hilariously at the Ahakista pub. "You're looking at it there across the water."

Options — swim (ha, ha) or go back the way we came, then drive 10, 11, 12 or even 13km past the hardware store where we'd last asked for directions.

"Then what do we do?" I asked. "You go to Ratooragh," the barman sighed.

"But we never passed any signposts!" I wheedled. "Oh, there's no signposts to Ratooragh," the barmaid interrupted in an if-one-more-fecking-tourist-comes-in-here-looking-for-their-roots-I'll-scream sort of a way.

"Two pints of Guinness, thanks miss."

Option three, of course, was to stay and play darts but, as the first one thrown landed on the floor just centimetres ("Jaysus, Paddy!") away from the foot of its thrower, it seemed safer to make polite chit-chat with the barmaid.

"It's just we're from New Zealand," I blathered, "and I'm looking for a relation of my mother's called Theresa Roberts, who lives with her cousin Mary Lucey somewhere near here in the area allegedly known as Ratooragh."

"Mary Lucey?" Well we should have said! Everybody knows Mary Lucey. Sure, just drive the 10, 11, 12 or even 13km past the town where we last asked for directions and then... stop and ask someone else.

Ten, 11, 12 or even 13km past the town, three men on three bikes herding three cattle beasts were holding up about 23 cars, which seemed like as good a time as any to step in a cow patty and ask if anybody knew the whereabouts of one Mary Lucey.

"Mary Lucey? Yes," the youngest of the three offered. "How to explain it?" He scratched his head. "Er. Um. Let me think. Right." He pointed to the only rooftop in sight. "Well, you see that house there? It's across the road from that."

As it happened, we were right on the cusp of Ratooragh or Rathura and didn't even know it, mostly because there doesn't seem to be anything there, hence the lack of signposts and absence from all but the most technical of diagrammatic representations.

Nothing except Connie and Mary Lucey's modest two-storey farmhouse, that is. Or so we assumed as we pulled the Punto into a muddy yard to the sound of at least a dozen barking dogs.

To be continued ...

More Irish Roots

HAVING FOUND the farmhouse which was allegedly home to my elderly Irish relative in windy West Cork, the ginger husband and myself were about to give up the trail. No one was answering the door and the cold was freezing our bits off.

Just then, though, a farmer appeared in the muddy yard.

"I'm looking for Mary Lucey," I explained.

"Yes," he replied.

"I'm from New Zealand and I'm a cousin of Theresa Roberts."

"Yes."

"Am I in the right place?"

"Yes."

"Are you Connie?"

"Yes."

For the past few years, Connie and his sister Mary have looked after Theresa Roberts, my great-grandmother's niece and the only surviving member of that particular branch of the Roberts family still living in Ireland.

Once he'd warmed to us a bit, Connie invited us into the little farmhouse to meet the famous Mary Lucey — it was asking for her by name which had led us to her doorstep when maps completely failed us.

"Ah sure and doesn't everybody know me since I was on the TV, winning the lottery," Mary laughed as she rustled around in a back room before re-emerging with a bottle of Baileys Irish Cream, a can of Heineken, a small bottle half-full of whiskey and a large, dusty bottle of cream sherry.

As she poured us each a huge vat of Baileys, she explained her grandmother had given her a bottle of whiskey when she was eight. She'd drunk the entire contents but the only effect it had had on her was she never wanted to drink again.

"Now come up and meet Theresa," Mary beckoned. "One at a time, so you don't frighten her."

Upstairs in a tiny, warm room, tucked into a toasty bed, was

97-year-old Theresa Roberts. Not too chipper, sure, but with the warmest hand you can imagine and all her marbles.

"What a grand pair," she said when the ginger husband joined me. (Told you she had all her marbles.)

While we visited, the doctor came and told Mary that, despite the fact Theresa had the heart of a 40-year-old, she should be taken to a nursing home by ambulance the next day, as she'd had nothing but a cup of tea all week.

We said our goodbyes to the gracious old lady but, before we continued our journey, we jumped in the car and Mary took us down the road to show us the remains of the old Roberts home. As a child, she'd loved visiting, because the Roberts had a gramophone and their own butter separator — which was still there, along with the dining table and what was left of a four-poster bed.

As we picked our way back down the muddy driveway towards our car, though, Mary suddenly grabbed my arm, her face completely stricken. "Oh, I never asked you did you want to use the toilet," she wailed. "Whatever will you think of our warm Irish hospitality?"

Driving back to drop her home, I assured her we were completely taken care of in the toilet department, had loved her hospitality and would treasure the memory of meeting the last of our Irish Roberts and the Luceys who so kindly cared for her.

"What a grand pair," Mary repeated as we finally went to take our leave. "Aren't they a grand pair?" she asked Connie. "Like movie stars," came the reply.

Now that's the sort of warm Irish hospitality a New Zealand relative could get used to. By the way, it was true about the lottery.

The City of Angels

UNTIL RECENTLY, I thought the only thing you could really love about the US was the fact it's very easy to buy little chocolatey things filled with peanut butter there.

I had a bad experience in Los Angeles some years ago involving a lot of Russian beer, my old pal, "Don't Travel With Me" Dave, and a biker with three ex-wives all called Sarah and a dangerous glint in his unfocused eye.

Since then, I've pretty much avoided the continent but, as I recently tricked the Ginger into okaying my "research" trip to the opposite side of the world, I slipped a 24-hour stopover in the City of Angels into my itinerary without him even noticing.

What you forget in a city the size and sprawl of LA is that you really need a cousin who has lived there for a few years and can squire you around the good bits and miss out the 65,000 or so square kilometres where nothing happens.

So, I'm fortunate in having Matthew, who picked me up at the airport in his VW bug and drove me immediately to the seaside settlement of Santa Monica for coffee.

The locals were rugged up in many layers of puffy clothing to ward off the chilly 15 degree C temperature. Oh, how I laughed.

At the coffee house, I was delighted to see there were three different people sitting alone at three different tables, working on three different laptops, no doubt on three practically identical screenplays.

I tried to get a closer look at one of them, imagining sitting in a cinema in three years time and, when the credits ran, gloating I'd practically slept with the scriptwriter.

However, there was much shouting and talk of calling the police and, what with the Russian beer and biker incident of 1990 and all, I sat down and drank my coffee instead.

By the way, "trim milk" is not an expression widely used in Santa Monica coffee bars. Nor is "cutlery".

Also sitting in the cafe at 8am were two perfectly coiffed

young gentlemen playing chess and obviously waiting to be discovered — I assume. Well, who blowdries their hair at that hour of the morning?

Delighted I had rubbed shoulders with the Hollywood wannabes, Matthew indulged me in my favourite thing to do in any city — driving around, looking at rich people's houses.

Margaritas at a Mexican hang-out were called for next, followed eventually by dinner at a restaurant where everybody had fabulous teeth and an air of being famous, even though none of them looked familiar. Another of my fears about the US was quashed when the portions turned out to be huge.

Back at Matthew and his wife Barbara's place, we ceremoniously ripped the scab off a bottle of Hawke's Bay merlot which I had secreted in my suitcase and drank a toast to home and away, Alexandra and LA, dogs and husbands and wives and, well, you know how it goes.

Next morning, I was dropped off at LA International Airport and, once they reopened the flight and stopped yelling at me, I was on my way to New York and not so much as a single peanut butter cup had crossed my mind — or lips.

The Big Apple

"START SPREADING the news," I sang to myself, as I arrived at JFK Airport. New York City. "I'm... yadda, yadda, yadda."

It was a cold Wednesday evening and I was nervous about being reunited with my luggage. Craning my neck over the crowds, I suddenly saw my 27kg of God-knows-what come toppling down the chute and made my way towards it, not quickly enough, however, to stop an old age pensioner from getting to it first.

She plonked it on her trolley and started heading out through Customs, while I banged and crashed my 42 bags of hand luggage through the milling hundreds, uselessly shouting, "Hey! Excuse me! Oi!"

Luckily for me, her hips weren't quite what they used to be and I was able to grab her before she absconded with my collection of black woolly clothes and computer cables.

This was a lesson — I was in the Big Apple and bad things could happen here.

Out on the cab rank, I clutched my handbag to my chest.

"Where to?" the cab driver asked.

"West Village. Corner of Hudson and Leroy. Two blocks north of Houston," I said efficiently, trying hard to act like I knew what I was talking about and hadn't practised it.

"That would be Howston, not Hewston," the cabby corrected me.

"Oh well, anything to make me sound like I'm not from New Zealand," I laughed.

"Noo Zealand?" he replied incredulously. "I tawt you was from the Bronx!" So began a lifelong (well, hour-long) friendship, during which I found out more about this guy than I could ever have imagined.

FOR EXAMPLE:

• He has two kids — son's a bit thick but daughter's a brainbox who's gonna have to go to a fancy college and where's

he going to get $30,000 a year for that?
- He talked to his wife about having another baby, only to find out she'd already been through menopause. "Can you believe that? Without me even noticing. So I say, 'Does this mean we don't need any protection? Let's go upstairs!'"
- He grew up in an Irish/Italian/Jewish part of Brooklyn, where his parents' travels caused quite some scandal. "Their first overseas trip, naturally, was to the Holy Land, but their second one was to Ireland and their neighbours are like, 'They're Jewish. What are THEY doing in Ireland?'"
- Want a great steak? You'd be wanting to go to Peter Lugers, in Brooklyn.
- He's writing a screenplay where the main character is, you guessed it, a New York cab driver.

Finally, after talking me through all the best landmarks of his lifetime, we were at the corner of Hudson and Leroy. We shook hands and parted, him promising to buy my book if he ever saw it and me promising to go to his film if I ever saw that. I'm telling you, if it hadn't cost me $40, it would have been once more around the block for sure.

Paris

I'VE BEEN TO PARIS once before, many years ago at New Year, and my most abiding memory is holding the back of someone's dress to stop her falling into the Seine while she brought up dinner and cheap chablis over the side of the city's oldest bridge.

Now that I'm far too mature and sophisticated for those kind of shenanigans, I thought since I was in London and they now have a train that goes under the sea to the French capital, I should get amongst it.

So I did. I met my friend in Burger King at Waterloo Station in London so we could fill up in case there wasn't any food in France and then we jumped on the train.

It whisked past the English countryside, everything went black for a bit, then it whisked past the French countryside and, all of a sudden, we were in Paris.

I immediately put the French lessons I had been giving myself at home in my car into practice.

"Ou est les bouteilles de vin blanc?" I asked an official-looking man in uniform.

"Queue up outside like everybody else," he said in a suspiciously Northern English sounding accent.

But the queue outside turned out to be for taxis and, as it was long and hardly moving, we decided to walk to our hotel, which looked pretty close on the map.

Harrumph. An hour later, we pulled our bags up to the Hotel Louvre Richlieu where, it seemed, two stars had dropped off since we'd booked it, leaving it with just one.

Still, I think flaky paint and drooping wallpaper is quaint, as it happens, especially when combined with constant traffic noise and petrol fumes.

We dumped our bags and set off to explore and, despite the rather industrial nature of our hotel's immediate surroundings, after a mere five minutes, we found ourselves in the forecourt of the Louvre, looking at acres of gorgeous garden with the Eiffel

Tower in the distance.

Stunned by the gorgeousness of it all, we sat down at the cafe across the road for a spot of staring at people.

I don't know how those French women do it. One after the other, they would walk by, shiny bobs popped on their heads, Chanel suits clinging to their tiny frames, classic heels lengthening their finely toned legs. A person could feel kind of frumpy in comparison. A person could start to think that wearing trainers and the same T-shirt for three days in a row was not particularly stylish.

But at least a person doesn't smoke any more and, with the bobbed brigade, a half-sucked gasper is still the accessory du jour, along with a pooch of course.

Many a whiskery-looking face could be seen poking out of a Prada handbag from a seat at the table next to you. I half expected them to smoke and order a cognac and all.

We broke up our bouts of people-watching by walking to the Eiffel Tower, spending an afternoon in the gardens of the Luxembourg Palace, brunching with the Parisians on the Left Bank on a Sunday morning and cruising the Seine to Notre Dame. To keep from fading away, we ate in little restaurants where the windows opened out on to flower boxes full of red geraniums, drank cafe au lait until it was coming out our ears and sampled the McCroque Monsieur.

The only minus to Paris from what I could see was that it smelt a bit of wees — but nothing to make you barf over a bridge or anything.

In my next life, I'm definitely going to be Juliette Binoche.

Irish Weather

I THOUGHT WE New Zealanders were obsessed with the weather but I can report to you, direct from the Emerald Isles, that the Irish are even worse.

It was the beginning of the Northern Hemisphere summer (early June) when I arrived in Dublin and the weather seemed horribly like that I had just left behind in Auckland.

Overcast, drizzly and sort of, well, a wee bit wintry.

"You've just missed the most amazing week!" my friend greeted me at the airport. "It's been blistering!"

Harumph. I had talked to her on the phone just days before leaving home and she had informed me that the conditions were, and I quote, "stone-splittingly hot".

Strangely, when I checked the paper that same day for the international temperatures, Dublin had recorded a high of just 14 degrees.

"You get OUR temperatures in YOUR paper?" she asked nervously when I told her — then applied some faux Irish logic claiming that the weather must have cooled on its way over to our measuring devices.

Still, she insisted that, right up until the moment my plane's wheels landed on the tarmac, eggs had been frying there — such was the heat.

I seem to remember this was the theme when we moved to Wellington for a while.

If I am to believe all accounts, it appears that wherever I am, the weather has just stopped being gorgeous and started being poxy. For my own sanity, I have to hope this isn't actually the case.

In Dublin, I started to wonder if my sanity had, in fact, been sucked out by too much airline food. Wherever I went, people were exhaling dramatically towards their fringes and fanning their faces in expressions of extreme over-heating.

At a high street cafe, I pulled my pashmina (Ha! I'll get another decade out of it if it kills me) tighter around my shoulders as a chill wind blew around my outdoor table.

No sooner had a young lad sat down opposite me than he started plucking his shirt away from his chest in a gesture of gross humidity. "Talk about muggy," he said, wiping imaginary sweat from his brow. "Beautiful day, isn't it?" the girl behind the counter beamed as I paid my bill. "Perfect!" grinned the old-timer sitting outside, grinning skyward. I started to wonder if *Candid Camera* was in town. Then I remembered an uncle coming back from a trip to Ireland when I was young. "The weather was beee-aa-uutiful," he said.

"It rained," said his wife.

"Only a little bit," said my uncle.

"Every day," said his wife.

"But it was beee-aa-uutiful rain," my uncle insisted.

"What does beautiful actually mean in weather terms?" I asked my Irish friend when I got back to her house after my coffee.

"Ah," she said, delighted I'd finally caught on. "Beautiful is not freezing cold and not raining."

"But still with clouds and wind?" I asked.

"Oh yes," she said. "No clouds, no wind, not freezing and not raining is blistering," she informed me. "And if it's actually hot as well, that's stone-splitting."

Upon not much reflection, I decided I far preferred this positively generous outlook towards the climate and immediately implemented it.

Ever since, as I have travelled the highways and byways of Ireland, researching my new novel — and not just fancying around on holiday as some gingery-type persons might claim — the weather has indeed gone from beautiful to blistering and, on one glorious occasion, even stone-splitting.

Perfect!

Nails

THE THING ABOUT a research trip to the cheesemakers of Ireland is that it is not complete without a three-day stopover in New York City on the way home. The logic behind this involves a lot of complicated diagrams and some long, drawn out calculations which I won't go into now but so it was that I found myself in Greenwich Village on the sofa bed of my friend Bridget, who has cleverly moved there.

Counting up what remained of my funny little New Zealand dollars at the end of a three-week trip, I realised I could either:

(a) buy a small farm in the South Island

(b) enjoy half a cup of someone else's coffee out of a nearby dumpster

(c) get a Manhattan manicure and pedicure.

The third option (mani-pedi as it is known) was, according to Bridget, the best time 20 bucks could buy a girl in New York.

Or the cheapest time anyway.

The only glitch was that I wouldn't normally consider myself a mani-pedi sort of a girl.

Mani-pedi girls, I have always imagined, do their hair every day instead of just on the day they wash it and don't try and eke their make-up out by wearing it three days in a row.

Mani-pedi girls' knickers are always clean on the same day as the matching bra and their eyebrows never meet in the middle just because the tweezers have never been the same since the bikini line incident of 1999.

Mani-pedi girls have small, tidy handbags which don't carry two litres of water, the latest Jackie Collins, trainers in case you get blisters from your nice shoes and an over-sized, nearly empty tube of embarrassing rash cream.

If mani-pedi girls are *Sex And The City*, I am strictly *Country Calendar*, so it was with some trepidation that I followed Bridget up the stairs to Soho Nails.

Inside, all along one wall, mani-pedi girls sat on raised thrones having their feet buffed by small crouching women on little footstools.

Upon being shown to my throne and slipping off my sandals, I suddenly felt the searing heat of two dozen pairs of eyes checking out my hooves.

Only then did I realise that I had Cookie-the-clown-like, boat-sized feet and toes that looked like yams. How could I have not noticed this before?

Too late to abandon ship, I swallowed my self-consciousness and miserably offered up my trotters to my own personal small crouching woman, only to become transfixed by the toes of the woman bethroned right next to me.

Sure, her handbag was small and Prada but her toenails were the size of dessert spoons. And on my other side? A bunion the size of Stewart Island. Hey, I thought, relaxing, the humble yam is looking pretty darn good right now.

The pedi consisted of a lot of soaking in water, a lot of nail clipping, a lot of stuff to do with cuticles and a foot massage that I had to pretend I wasn't enjoying as much as I was for fear they would kick me out for lewd behaviour.

This was topped off with three layers of Bordeaux nail polish with a bunch of loo paper wound around the toes to stop them mingling with each other.

Then I was slipped into a pair of cardboard slippers and sent to mani where the whole wonderful process was repeated, with my hands and fingernails.

Weeks later, I'm still reliving that magical hour-and-a-half. I may be uncoordinated in the knicker and bra department but I'm a mani-pedi girl through and through.

Modern Girls

Girly Weekends

WHAT DO YOU GET when you cross a cheesy motel with four grown women and a boot full of wine? A girls' weekend away, of course. (Okay — sometimes a migraine.)

Everyone deserves at least one girls' weekend away a year (if not seven) but, if it has been a while for you, I am recently returned from one and can refresh your memory on how they work.

The bossiest among you chooses the time and the place and the rest of you simply turn up, moaning and bitching about the funny smell and the swirly carpet but otherwise happy to have escaped the home front.

Cups of tea are dispersed and the topic of what you are going to do next is broached.

This starts with talk of horse-riding, moves on to go-karting, lingers a while on Bobby from *The Practice*, continues with a quickly pooh-poohed suggestion of a hill climb and ends approximately where it started, only much later in the day.

Luckily, by that stage, it's time for a tipple.

"A small vat of chardonnay," you cry. "I'll just sip it."

I have vague memories — you'll soon understand why — from my early twenties of a girls' weekend away, which started in a rambling hotel in the Blue Mountains of New South Wales and finished in the accident and emergency room of the local hospital, with 64 glasses of port in between (there were four of us).

Once the first cork pops, the real gossip starts.

First, you trash all the girls who said they were going to come but didn't. Then, you decide who among you is the thinnest and are mean to her for a while. Next, you establish who is the oldest and offer sympathy, while secretly feeling glad it's not you — unless it is you, in which case you start being mean to the thin person again.

The talk will eventually turn to what you are having for

dinner, which will be something light and healthy, because there's no need to let standards slip, just because you're on holiday.

You'll try on each other's clothes, linger on Bobby from *The Practice* again, then trash all your husbands.

Someone will admit they tongue-kissed your boyfriend back in the early 1980s and a small fight will break out.

More corks will pop and you will all cry and say how much you love each other. No, you really, really love each other. You mean it.

Then you'll order pizza — lots of it — and garlic bread.

By the time the food arrives, the crying will be finished and you will all be dancing. The crying might start up again now but it will only be the pizza delivery boy, begging to be set free.

More corks will pop, then suddenly you'll be on the phone, sobbing to the aforementioned dead-beat of a husband he's the best thing to ever happen to you — and what does it matter what the time is? Then you'll put down the phone, only to ring him again immediately, forgetting you already did.

Next thing you know, it's morning and you're talking about whether abseiling or mince pies will get rid of your headache. The bossiest among you is making you write down the next time and place — and you can't wait.

Baby Waxing

I SUPPOSE I SHOULD have thought it suspicious no one has ever suggested to me having your legs waxed and looking after a baby are two great things to do together.

It seemed like such a good idea at the time.

My sister and I both get different bits of our legs waxed (between us, we make up a complete set) so I suggested the mobile waxer come and kill two birds with one pot of boiling hot hair-ripper-outer.

The plan was, while Anna was having her legs waxed, I would look after her little boys and, while I was having my legs waxed, well, who cared what happened to them then? They're not mine, after all.

Like many a good hair removal episode, this one went horribly wrong horribly early.

Anna was called away to a meeting, the waxer arrived early, the sleeping baby woke up and started squawking.

Enter the Ginger.

"Here, take this," I said, thrusting a sobbing 10-month-old Hugo into his arms.

"How do you turn it down?" he asked, holding the poor creature at arm's length.

"Sing to it," I said over my shoulder before recalling the Ginger's recent rendition of *Stairway to Heaven*. "Erm, play air guitar to it."

Minutes later, I was on the slab in a separate room having hot wax applied to my calves.

The sound of Hugo not being impressed reverberated around the walls.

"He'll be fine, really," I said to the waxer. "My sister will be home any minute. It's okay. Would you call that crying or screaming? It's nothing. Don't you think? Actually, just one moment please."

I jumped off the bed and hobbled out to the living room.

The Ginger was sitting on the sofa with Hugo on his knee. They were staring at each other and both looking sad but only one was crying.

"Walk around! Jiggle!" I hissed.

"More of a whimper than a howl," I reported to the waxer as I leapt back on the bed and she commenced wrenching.

"Quite loud for a whimper though, eh?" I laughed.

"So where do you think the word hysterical actually came from? I'm sorry, I'll be back in a jiffy."

Partly deforested, I hobbled again into the living room, where I happened upon the Ginger holding the still wailing Hugo above his head.

"He weighs a bloody ton," the Ginger said, depositing the baby in my arms and snatching his car keys. "See you."

Before I could yell a single instruction at him, he was gone. Hugo stopped crying and squeezed out a little smile.

"I suppose it's important for them to know about the pain we suffer to maintain our gorgeous exteriors," I said to the waxer as Hugo sat on my lap and she waxed around him.

"I think he likes it," she suggested and, sure enough, didn't the dear wee mite giggle and laugh every time she ripped another strip of hair out.

When Anna finally got home with three-year-old Angus, it took quite some explaining why Auntie S K was sitting in her nana knickers covered in wax and clutching a baby brother.

The depilatory concept obviously got him thinking.

"Did the lady take all your hair off?" Angus asked as I made to leave. "Cos you've still got some on your head."

Swearing

I HEARD SOMEONE say, the other day, swearing is a sign of poor character which means, being ever so slightly foulmouthed, I'm just as skint in character as I am in everything else.

Not that I believe in effing and blinding just for the sake of it. Not at all.

I just feel in some instances, obscenities are absolutely appropriate and should be hurled with great venom and volume.

Driving along the highways and byways of Auckland, for example, one gets ample opportunity to vent one's spleen at the selfishness and gall of other drivers.

Why, with the windows wound up and the car radio on, I can swear myself hoarse in a mere five-kilometre stretch of the North-Western, leaving my vocabulary pearly white and sparkling for the rest of the day.

I have special phrases for people who cut in without indicating, a number of words for those who drive slowly in the fast lane, a matching gesture for tail-gaters and, for those who don't wave after you let them in in front of you, words hardly do those ingrates justice, but I come pretty close with my handcrafted, purpose-built string of invective, I tell you.

Toe stubbing is another time when swearing is appropriate, especially if you keep stubbing the same toe on the same thing. "Ouch" just doesn't get you anywhere. Nor does, "Clever bed leg. Still there, eh?"

A curse, expelled loudly with at least a dozen invisible exclamation marks and a lot of hopping about, is all that helps ease the pain.

As for getting four hours up country before remembering the dog is tied to a tree outside your house waiting to be loaded into the car? Just try a "Silly me!" on for size and see how it fits.

There are, of course, times when swearing is totally inappropriate and you can only hope the first time you meet your in-laws-to-be you are not in a car, near a bed leg, or mistakenly minus your pooch.

Obviously, any room or vehicle which has a small child in it, too, should be effing and blinding free, and that's for your own sake.

Strangely, at point blank, the little brats can't hear you tell them to pick up their toys yet, from a distance of several kilometres will hang onto your every word beginning with "f" and a few beginning with "b".

Then the little gnomes, while not displaying enough intelligence to tie their own shoelaces, will take all those "f" and "b" words and rearrange them into a sentence about Auntie Maude which they will practise on her the moment she steps off the bus from Hawera where there are apparently no "little guttersnipes".

It is a worry, I admit, how the really terrible swear words have become less terrible. I can clearly remember the first time I heard THE "f" word and it had me racing to the confessional in my St Mary's uniform — and I hadn't even said it myself.

These days, a girl would be wearing a track to the church and looking pretty silly in a gymslip to boot.

The good news is there don't seem to be any brand new really terrible swear words so any moment now we can start recycling the old ones and maybe, accidentally, we'll end up wholesome again.

Gadzooks! Wouldn't that be something?

The Economy

IF YOU HEAR about anything going down in price, please let me know because all this doom and gloom is turning my normally sunny disposition to the south.

For a start, I can't afford to fill my car up with gas any more and I haven't been in straits quite so dire since the Dexter years of the early 1980s.

Dexter was my 1961 Hillman Minx station wagon (rego AU2555, in case he's still alive) and he and I lived through a rough patch when the kind ladies of the Manawatu Budgeting Service had me on such strict rations I could only afford $2.50 of gas at any one time.

This meant Dexter would quite often run out of juice between destinations and I would have to abandon him at the roadside. Cleverly I kept my 10-speed bicycle in the back so I would usually get where I was going to anyway, only slower.

Eventually Dexter lost all control of reverse, first and second gears, which made backing out of angle parking quite impossible and the good folk of Palmerston North soon tired of me driving along the footpath looking for an opening back out on to the street.

Finally I was reduced to selling Dexter for rubble for the princely sum of $250 only to see him some months later flying past me at great speed on a motorway, repainted purple and looking quite full of himself.

Those were the days, eh? Try putting $2.50 in your car now. You probably inhale that much gas just waiting for the nine-year-old forecourt attendant to stop picking his nose and amble over from the magazine rack.

Really it's enough to make you turn to smoking. Oh, hang on. That's out of the question now the poisonous sticks have rocketed to nearly a tenner a pack.

Unless, that is, you can get your gaspers duty free on the way back from your overseas trip.

Overseas trip? Well, with the New Zealand dollar being worth approximately two pebbles and a fingernail clipping, that trip to Fiji is definitely on the back-burner. Did I say Fiji? Really where is my head?

I was discussing my limited understanding of our economy (technical opinion: sucks a big kumara) with an old friend I bumped into in the supermarket the other day.

He was very good at maths at school and now works at something sort of governmental involving numbers.

His advice was if the doom and gloom of it all gets too much for you, try reading what the Reserve Bank has to say because it's usually its fault things have turned to mush anyway and hence it is obliged to shine a favourable light on it all.

What appears to the average Joe to be brown and squashy and not at all pleasant to sniff comes up smelling of roses, by all accounts.

Of course, the Reserve Bank quarterly report is hardly going to be a bodice ripper but might help with stacking the zeds if paying $60 for a tank of gas is keeping you awake at night.

The alternative to this, which I am trialling at the moment, is to go daily to see *The Patriot* at the North City cinema complex, where I am asked every time without fail if I am 15.

When times are tough it's the little things you cling to.

Book Clubs

I FOOLISHLY pooh-poohed the Tupperware craze but I'm not going to miss out on a fad like that again, so I have joined a book club.

These are the Tupperware parties of the new millennium. Groups of six to 10, usually women, gather at one or other's house of a given evening once a month to discuss a previously designated book. These discussions range from deeply intelligent analysis of the plot and text to roaring hysteria over thinly related topics — someone's husband's holey underpants, for instance. I'd been desperate to join a book club for ages but no one had invited me, so I did the sensible thing — I invited myself to a friend's one.

I was so excited it's hard to understand why I didn't bother reading the actual book. I knew about it for weeks in advance. I had a copy. I'd started it (six or seven times). But as book club night drew nearer, I strangely seemed drawn only to magazines and free advertising matter. Then, just days before the big night, I remembered it was "ladies-a-plate".

Well, I was in such a tizzy that I had no time for reading a 600-page book in 48 hours, anyway. What would I take? I didn't know these people. If I went to too much trouble, they'd think I was flashy. If I bought chocolate chip cookies from the supermarket, they'd think I was cheap. If I bought anything too complicated to construct, I'd spend the whole night in the kitchen. Worst of all, I had no sensible container to contain whatever I was taking, owing to the whole Tupperware pooh-poohing disaster of the late 20th century.

"Take the salmon dippy thing," the Ginger suggested, thrilled to pieces I would be leaving him for a whole night so he could watch motorsport on TV and scratch himself in peace.

I arrived at the book club with a little dish of dip, a loaf of bread and a deep, deep desire not to be asked anything about the book in question. By the way, has anybody ever noticed that, if you're in a real hurry, the cling film doesn't cling, yet if you've all the time in the world it sticks like glue? What's that all about?

Anyway, introductions were made, the comestibles circulated and the deeply intelligent analysis began.

"This dip is really good," came the first comment.

"The spring rolls are delicious — have you tried them?"

"Soup? Or should we save ourselves for dessert?"

In other words, only one person had finished the book. She told us what happened and we agreed none of us needed to finish it, as she'd done such a sterling job and, oh, I will have another glass of that sauvignon blanc, thank you.

Bloody good night and so stimulating!

In fact, so flushed am I by the success of my first book club that I thought I might join another one or 27. Not only shall I feast like a king every night but some clubs are mixed, so it's "gentlemen-a-plate" as well, which should be interesting.

And of course there is the small matter of my own novel coming out towards the end of the year. According to my calculations, if I infiltrate a book club a week between now and November, recommending my own tome as I go, what I make in extra book sales will just about cover the salmon dip.

Changing Rooms

HELP ME, I've been traumatised by one changing room too many. I'm sure they're getting smaller — it can't just be me. Hang on, let me think about that for a moment — better have some Gingernuts and a couple of sausage rolls to help the thought process... No, it can't just be me.

I can't count the number of times I've bent over to pick something up, banged my head on the mirror then reared back with the pain of it, only to push open the door with my butt and expose myself to unsuspecting shoppers and at least three salespeople chorusing, "All right in there, are we?"

But I think it's getting worse.

The latest changing room to scar me psychologically was everything you expect in a cubicle — too small, too hot, not enough hooks for the hangers, mirrors which make you look spottier than you were when you were 13, nothing to put your bag on and very bright lights.

On top of that, though, the curtain stopped too soon.

This I discovered when I saw myself in someone else's cubicle across the way and realised that, what with the winter and the cold and all, I had been a bit remiss on the armpit hair front.

The woman in whose mirror my armpits were doing their small furry animal impersonations noticed too.

Then we both realised armpits oughtn't to be viewed from a cubicle other than one's own, at which stage it became clear the cubicle curtain was not high enough.

While short people, shaved people, children and hobbits would have loved them, a person of stature like myself couldn't help but think that, if I jumped up and down a bit, other customers would get quite an eyeful and most likely not feel much like shopping any more.

I registered my deep disapproval of the insubstantial cubicle curtain by saying absolutely nothing and going to the supermarket to buy some disposable razors.

At least it wasn't communal, I thought with a shudder. I'm still taking pills to get over those.

A few months ago, I sensibly chose a boiling hot sunny day to go shopping for brassieres.

Predictably, all the ones I liked looked like the incredible hulk was bursting out of them, while all the ones which fitted had straps a mile wide and could have formed the outer shells for a string of hospitals in the Himalayas, such was their substance.

After about an hour, hot and crabby and unsatisfied in a tiny cubicle which gave me far too good a view of my rear end, I conceded defeat and gave up. But while loitering in the bargain bin, picking over cheap undies on my way out of the store, I was approached by a nervous saleswoman.

"Excuse me," she stammered. "I think this might be yours." She handed me something grey and tatty and slightly familiar — my own brassiere, in fact.

Somehow it had slipped through the net of my getting dressed procedure and had made a break for freedom, wheedling its way into the huge pile of spurned underthings due to be returned to the shelves.

I, meanwhile, was walking around unaware and, even worse, unharnessed.

I blame the changing room entirely but you'll be happy to know I have now implemented a checklist to make sure I have all my clothes on in the right order whenever I leave a stuffy cubicle. Or home. Or any other place where confusion of this kind can crop up.

The Sound of Music

BEFORE YOU READ any further, there's something you need to know about me. Something you may not like. Something I have been keeping from you.

I am a *Sound of Music* fan.

As a girl, I'd come home from kindy and listen to Julie Andrews on the record player, while sipping a nice cup of tea.

As a teenager, I learned to hide my love of Maria and her clan behind a veneer of faked devotion to Neil Diamond, Queen and Supertramp.

As a young adult, I chose the middle ground of Madonna, Simply Red and those Mexicans who sang *Bambilaya* or whatever it was.

As an old adult, however, I can hide my true feelings no longer. For this reason, on my recent international sojourn, I eschewed the tourist traps of Los Angeles, New York and Dublin in favour of the Von Trapps of Leicester Square, courtesy of the Sunday afternoon *Singalonga-Sound of Music* at the Prince Charles (no relation) theatre.

Myself and a coven of Julie fans met outside the cinema, along with a throng of nuns, girls in white dresses with blue satin sashes and men in lederhosen.

For those who hadn't made a little something out of their bedroom curtains to compete in the half-time lookalike competition, there was the *Sound of Music* singalong pack.

This contained a headkerchief, some edelweiss, a foam rubber nun for sticking your fingers through and waving, streamers for the party scene and throat lozenges.

Before the movie started, the MC gave a quick run down of all the movements to *Do-Re-Mi*, then made sure everybody knew you raised both hands to the heavens when you heard the word "hills"; you go "ahhh" when you see the little Von Trapps; you boo the Nazis; hiss the Baroness; and, at the sight of the telegram boy, bark like a dog.

The rest of the time you sing along to all your favourites, helped by the words in huge letters on the screen.

Cinema-goers chatted happily through the film, silencing themselves only in anticipation for the big musical numbers.

Real fans shouted out the dialogue before Julie got to it and, when poor Maria was told by the mean old captain she couldn't have any material to make play clothes for the children, the entire audience shouted, "Behind you! Behind you!", until she finally turned and fingered the drapes in a thoughtful fashion.

Julie's performance, however, took second place to the looka-like contest at halftime.

Usually, there's a separate contest for all the nuns but, on this occasion, they were all in the bar sculling lager like there was no tomorrow, so a seven-year-old with a T-shirt on her head was the only entrant.

Add to that two Baronesses, the head of the Nazis, a handful of Marias, a collection of unrelated Von Trapps, the woman who comes third in the talent quest (known as "Bowing Lady") and six matching bees from Brighton (think *Favourite Things*) and you've got the picture.

The winner? Two brown paper packages tied up with string, who'd come all the from Birmingham on the train.

Laugh? Hardly a dry seat in the house.

Columnists

I DON'T USUALLY watch TV3's *Sex in the City*, because it reminds me too much I don't have a life.

The more the four sexy starlets who feature in the show run around looking gorgeous and bonking handsome studs, the more I sit on the sofa in my track pants, wishing it was on at 8.30pm instead of 9.30pm, so I could be in my bed already.

How come they can always be bothered going out at night? Don't they worry they'll feel tired the next day? And what's with having a different cocktail frock for every night of the week? Don't they know it makes those of us still re-dying our wedding dresses feel bad?

Still, sometimes the swearing in *The Sopranos* on TV2 gets too much even for me and I switch over.

"Oh, look," said the Ginger last time I did this, pointing at Sarah Jessica Parker on the telly as she lay on her bed in tiny knickers, tapping away at a laptop. "She's a columnist, just like you."

Oh, how I laughed. Yes, I told him. We're practically twins. People get us mixed up all the time. Oh no, hang on. I got that wrong. Actually, apart from the fact we both breathe oxygen, we don't have a single thing in common. And, for all I know, she doesn't even breathe oxygen. It probably fills her up too much.

"A-ha," shouted Ginge, with a glint in his eye. "She has a pashmina and so do you."

What can I say? He still has "issues" with my Visa bill.

Yes, I pointed out, but did you notice she has one in every colour known to man and can wrap hers three times around her neck, whereas my lonely little eggshell blue number barely makes it around once?

What with that apartment, her spangly midriff tops and the hair product and all, she must be earning a fortune writing her column, I continued.

"Well, she probably doesn't spend much on food," the Ginger

countered, before falling to the ground, clutching his head where a large plate of macaroni cheese seemed to have struck it.

After torturing him for a few hours with a pot of honey and the curling tongs, he eventually agreed Sarah Jessica Parker made being a columnist look far too easy and fun.

In real life, it is actually quite hard work which only a very clever person who eats three full meals a day and wears substantial underpants can manage.

Of course, Richard Gere did nothing for our image in the movie *Runaway Bride*, where he spends approximately four seconds at his computer and six months chasing Julia Roberts, whom he, of course, eventually marries.

Yes, that's happened to me several times. I've turned Julia Roberts down twice, actually.

"Nothing like you," the Ginger yelled nervously, when Nick Nolte showed up on our TV screen the other night, playing yet another loafing columnist in the crappy movie, *I Love Trouble*.

All he did (once he finished his smokin', drinkin' and womanisin', that is), was get his secretary (ha!) to look up what he wrote about at the same time last year, change a few key words and the date, press a button and hey presto. Less than a minute's work.

As if you could get away with that in real life. Disgusting.

Next week, the modern girl's guide revisits the smorgasbord.

Personalised Plates

EVERY TIME I SEE a personalised number plate, I wonder if the driver of the car bought it for themselves or if it was a gift.

Then, I wonder, if it was a gift, how did the recipient feel about it? Did they love it? Did they rush outside and bang it straight on their car? Did they wonder what they had ever seen in this person? Did they kick them in the shins and run away screaming?

Take something like SHLEEZ, for example. When I see something like that, I wonder if someone sleazy with a shpeech impediment bought it for themselves or if a lovestruck boyfriend had to settle for it as a gift, because SHELLY had already been taken.

Myself, I have no desire to own a personalised plate, although the Ginger is often threatening to buy me LRDRS for a birthday present.

"Not unless you want to see it coming towards you at great speed," I laughed shrilly, adding that, nevertheless, it would be better than buying me a Swiss Army knife which can perform gynaecological surgery but has no corkscrew, which is what I got for Christmas.

Oh, how he laughed when I took his car to the garage for him and got sent home in a courtesy car called SCOOTA.

Suddenly, I found myself under the scrutiny of other personalised plate watchers. Did they think I was SCOOTA? Or did they perhaps think someone else thought I was a SCOOTA? Did I look like a SCOOTA? Did I look like someone who did not want to look like a SCOOTA?

I remembered the time we'd stopped at a country cafe and a MUFFY was parked outside. I quickly placed a bet, claiming I would be able to spot the MUFFY owner within one minute but, upon entering the coffee shop, was confronted with a clientele made up almost exclusively of hairy truck drivers. Surely, not a MUFFY among them.

By the same token, I felt a certain lack of baseball hats left me not looking very SCOOTA-ish.

Actually, the first personalised plate I can ever remember seeing, in Wellington more than a decade ago, remains my favourite. RSWIPE used to park around the corner from where I lived and cheered me up enormously every time I saw it, although obviously you have to really like toilet paper humour to appreciate it. Since then, I'm sure New Zealand has accumulated more personalised plates per head of population than any other country, which is quite good because we probably have more excellent six-letter-or-less expressions than other places, too. (GIDDAY, BUGGER and, another personal favourite, AS U DO, among them. Haven't spotted GR8 M8 or 4NIC8 as yet.) On any half-hour straight of motorway in the country, you can usually clock up at least an AV8R, an XLR8, an ONEDGE, a couple of FOXY or FOXEEs, a DAZZR, a BAZZR, a GAZZR and one or other of IM PHIL, BILL or JILL.

Another half-hour and you'll see probably four or five variations on CRUISN, including the truck who obviously got there last, CRUZN, not under pain of death, no doubt, no matter what the temptation, to be rhymed with "cousin".

Of course, after more than an hour, if you're obsessed with correct punctuation the way I am, you have to give up on the plate spotting, because it will drive you around the twist and not in a good way.

RIGHTO, BETRGO. CUL8R, LIG8R.

Baches

NEXT TO IT being okay to be pear-shaped, the best thing about being a Kiwi has to be the bach.

Nowhere else I've been to (all right, so that's only the left-hand corner of Ireland, the bottom bits of England and one drop in the pool of Australia) seems to relish the same style of simplified holiday-making.

Thus, it can be quite hard to describe the concept of baches to visiting foreigners.

"Oh, you know," you'll say, as they look at you, bewildered, "it's like a crib — only in the North Island".

"So, this 'batch' you speak of — how many in each one?" they'll ask, dislodging the stone between their sock and sandal.

You'll go all dreamy-eyed and start reminiscing over the first bach you ever stayed in. Most likely, it was somewhere your dad organised through a mate at work, which wasn't in the spot all your friends were staying in, by the lake, but about 10km out of town, on the back of someone's farm.

You'll find yourself recalling the old Valiant being loaded with chilly bins and sleeping bags and charcoal for the barbie and your ears will ring with the same screaming argument you had with your mother every year at holiday time.

"Why can't I have jandals?"

"Because they give you blisters between your toes and you always lose them."

"All of the other kids have got them."

"If all the other kids jumped off a cliff, would you jump, too?"

Once you arrived at the bach, there'd be lots of running inside and opening and closing doors, checking out how many kids to a room and if there was a bath or not. Showers rule.

The true Kiwi bach must satisfy a few criteria or it becomes some other sort of holiday home. A chalet or something.

For a start divans with drawers are better than bunks. Things which fold out from the walls are better than things which don't fold out from the walls. A wringer washing machine, like the one that kid at school broke his arm in, is better than nothing at all.

The bach must not have fancy flooring. Lino, floorboards and concrete are fine — terracotta tiles are not.

The bach must have restricted bench space in the kitchen and an element which only goes on full bore. There must only be one cooking utensil, preferably with a melted handle, and under no circumstances must there be a wooden spoon. Hyperactive children on holidays, mothers with not enough bench space and wooden spoons spell only one thing — pants down, bottoms smacked — and this is too much like being at home.

Another thing which separates the bach from whatever it is Australians have holidays in (Asia?) is the games collection.

This consists of a 1960s version of either Monopoly or Cluedo. If it's Cluedo, the lead pipe will have been replaced by a matchstick and, if it's Monopoly, the top hat will be a thimble or a toothpaste lid. There will not be enough money in the bank.

Any pack of cards found in the games drawer or cupboard will be missing the ace of spades. This will not be discovered until the day before you leave, at which stage your fat-head big sister will have to relinquish her "Queen of Cards" crown, because it didn't bloody count, did it?

The true Kiwi bach, no matter how old you get and how many different ones you go to, never, ever changes.

Knitting

IT MUST BE WINTER because I've started knitting. This is something which happens once a year, lasts a couple of months and never ends in a completed article of clothing.

This worries me not a lot, because I find the clickety-clack of knitting needles quite therapeutic and shouting obscenities at the complicated instructions a great way to ward off the winter chill.

The ginger husband, on the other hand, has a great big bee in his bonnet about finishing everything you start.

"But it's nice to have a hobby," I wheedled, when I arrived home with the latest plastic bag stuffed with mohair and needles. "And don't they say it's not finishing which is important it's making it to halfway? It's the putting right that counts? Or something like that?"

I was about to give him the full treatment about not stifling my creative urges when he disappeared into the cavernous hole under the stairs and emerged an hour or so later, covered in cobwebs and staggering under the weight of a large crate of partially formed knitwear.

Turns out it's quite some collection, which includes two-thirds of a cardigan, half a scarf, one sock, nearly all of a mitten, the beginnings of a beanie and something which started off being a tie and finished up being the dog's favourite thing to try to mate with.

The Ginger will never understand one of the best things about knitting is trying to find a pattern where the woman on the cover looks like someone who doesn't still live at home with her mother and wear socks and Roman sandals together.

It's a dying art these days, now completely knitted-up and finished and ready-to-wear type woollens are so cheap to buy. I'm actually just doing my own little bit to help keep the universe turning the way it always has.

No, well, the Ginger didn't fall for that either.

The truth is that in the dark, cold months of the year, one can spend far too much time worrying about how *Shortland Street* would get patients if the staff didn't all eventually wind up in there. Or what chance Ena Sharples would have of getting a milk stout at the Rovers these days. Or why, as soon as you finally remember what night all your favourite programmes are on, the schedule changes. Or how much more you like Alison from *Melrose Place* now she's on *Ally McBeal* even though she's still married to someone with the annoying name of Billy.

In other words, TV can take over a girl's life and it's good to have the distraction of dropping stitches and poking your eye out with a needle to keep yourself in real life.

This winter, I am not even limiting myself to knitting something I'd actually wear even if I did finish it, which is why I am one-sixteenth of the way through a matching midriff top and mini skirt in lilac and lemon stripes. Size eight.

In the summer — when I can't see the telly, because of the glare — I'm going to buy a lot of fabric and sewing patterns and pin and cut things out a lot.

One year, I actually finished something. Well, almost finished. I never did get the hang of button-holes, which is a real shame because I've bought a lot of very nice buttons in my time.

Sleep

WHAT IS IT about sleep which makes it so delicious? After all, pretty much nothing exciting happens unless some prankster sticks your hand in a jug of warm water or you have the good luck to dream about having sex with someone famous and being congratulated for your dexterity afterwards.

Mostly, though, you just lie there like a big lump, snoring slightly and scratching yourself. Sometimes there may even be flatulence or drool. There may be caked-on mascara. Your hair could look as though the dog has been digging in it for a week. Your breath could be hazardous to flammable products.

Chances are, "glamour" will not be the first word which springs to mind when you look at yourself in the mirror upon waking.

Yet, despite all this ugliness and hideosity, I continue to make it my life's mission to get more sleep.

This could have something to do with currently working at a job where the alarm goes off before the little hand hits six. I have never been good in this zone. A mean, ornery, scary lady with a very deep voice like Arnold Schwarzenegger inhabits my body in this zone and often makes me stub my toe and swear to boot.

When I wake in the before-six zone, my first thoughts are of being back asleep again. I immediately start to imagine going to bed and getting more sleep and this propels me through those first difficult moments of the morning.

What a go-getter, eh? How times have changed. In my twenties, I avoided sleep like the plague. If I got more than five hours a night, I was lucky and there had to be at least one all-nighter a week or I'd feel downright frumpy.

At one stage in the mid 1980s, I had a job which started when the little hand hit five and, on one particular occasion I can remember getting home at 4.07am and setting the alarm for 4.45am. You know, the same day.

I tell you, the very thought of getting just 38 minutes sleep of a night now has me reaching for the smelling salts and swooning.

I don't think it's just old age which has me permanently eyeing up the scratcher, though. I could blame the Ginger. Well heck, since he's there, I may as well.

He's always wanted more sleep than I and, in the early years of our union, he could often be found snoring on the sofa at a friend's house while everybody else stayed up past 10 o'clock chatting and putting away a few chardonnays.

Similarly, at home, guests would get used to him quietly excusing himself and disappearing, never to be seen again.

When there was no one at home except the two of us, he would beg to be allowed to go to bed early but I would only allow it once he had completed a complicated series of chores like foot rubs, hot chocolates and menial housework.

For about a decade and a half, his obsession with being conked out really got up my nose.

Then, suddenly, I noticed what a nice person he was in the morning. No ugly black bags. No eye-watering obscenities. No crying and pleading for just five more minutes.

Our bed started speaking to me in words only I could hear and, before I knew it, I was planning my sleep days in advance and even sleeping in sympathy for other people who weren't getting enough of their own. You know, like parents.

Now it's me performing unusual acts so I can hit the hay in time to get my eight hours' worth. And I tell you one thing — the next husband I get will have smaller feet.

Sisters

WHILE FOR THE PURPOSES of more and better presents I have often dreamed of being an only child, I am actually lucky enough to have two sisters.

I'm the eldest, then there's a taller one and, much later on, there's a little, thin one.

Sometimes we have to tie her to a tree, force feed her kettle-fried crisps and beat her with a stick until she begs for rich, chocolate ice-cream.

Being something of an autumn leaf, she's substantially younger than we are, so we have to give her an extra kick in the shins every now and then for that, too.

The tall one has given me two gorgeous nephews, Bang-Bang and Choppy, for which I am extremely grateful. The young one has just graduated from Victoria University with Honours in Law, so I'm pretty much hoping she will become extremely rich and support me in my dotage despite the thrashings.

This might just work out okay, as she has always been quite good at taking orders. Sort of.

When she was very little, people used to sometimes think she was my baby — perhaps because I was tall for my age. Some people are thick. I mean, I'm sure there were some 13-year-old mums around in those days but I doubt they played witches and fairies and liked maths homework the way I did.

Eventually, in a fit of rebellion, I decided to deliberately pretend she was my baby in a bid to try and shock the old crumblies at the local mall.

Although she probably wasn't even two yet, I thought she was terribly clever and outlined my plan with her outside the wool shop, where I figured the biggest collection of shockable old biddies would be gathered.

"Wait outside until I get up to the counter, then run in, crying, 'Mamma, Mamma'," I told her.

No sooner had I struck up a conversation about four-ply with the shop assistant than the clever creature, a glint in her eye, ran straight for me, crying loudly and clearly, "Nana, Nana".

A teenage mum the knitting brigade might have believed but I needed more than height to make it into Nanaville. Little pest.

I've forgiven her now I realise she may well finance my twilight years in a suite at the McDonald's Golden Arches Home for the Carbohydrate-Addicted. I'm just disappointed you have to be older than 38 to move in.

Speaking of moving in, did I mention we have bought an empty rectangle in the city and are hoping to turn it into a flat? Sadly for us, the Wellington City Council believes lots of men with pocket protectors wearing socks and sandals together have to hike into the hills with only a sausage roll between them to decide whether we should be allowed to erect three internal walls.

Obviously, the vegetarians in the group became weak with hunger and slowed the others down, while their plastic-soled sandals became slippery on the muddy slopes of the capital's steep terrain.

Leastways, they're taking their time coming back with such a difficult decision.

This leaves myself, my ginger husband, our dog and two carloads full of supplies a little short on the housing front now we are headed back to Wellington and our empty rectangle is still an empty rectangle.

Unless... well, there's always the little sister's room at home. It wouldn't be for long and, besides, she may as well get used to accommodating us.

Doing It Yourself

Rectangles

UP TO THE EYEBALLS with hearing me moan on and on about moving around from pillar to post, the Ginger has bought us an apartment.

Well, when I say apartment, I really mean room. And when I say room, I really mean that's probably what it wants to be when it grows up.

"Walk me through it," a friend said excitedly on the phone, when I rang to tell her the news.

"Well, you open the front door and that's it," I explained.

"Don't be ridiculous," she snorted. "There must be more to it than that."

"Two of the walls are longer than the other two," I replied after thinking about it for a bit.

"Oh, so it's a rectangle!" she cried excitedly. "You see — I knew there was more to it!"

Once I got Pollyanna off the phone, I faced the grim reality that, because the Ginger was working around the clock sticking fake fur on hobbits, or whatever it is he does, I was in charge of turning the rectangle into somewhere to live.

I drew up a list of things I thought it needed but after three days, I still only had two written down. Kitchen. And bathroom.

It's an empty rectangle.

"So where exactly does one buy a bathroom, then?" I casually asked the Ginger over tea and toast. "For around, say, the $9.50 mark?"

After a lot of muttering about doing it yourself and renting not being so bad after all, I eventually deciphered he thought the phone book was a good place to start, so I thanked him kindly for his assistance and suggested he might not chew so carefully in the future because a good choke might be in order.

After eight hours of pricing toilets, I felt the claw-like clench of constipation grip my innards. "How can a lav possibly go from costing $200 to $2000?" I wondered.

"For that money," I told the pimply youth in the shop, as I pointed at their superior model, "I'd want a colonic irrigation plus flowers and a movie. Every time."

"You'd want to have very fast-moving bowels to make that one worthwhile," I told the manager, as he attempted to usher me out the door.

"All that money for one regular motion a day?" I shouted, as his henchmen threw me out on the street. "I don't think so."

At the oven shops of the city, I became similarly confused. Nobody seemed to think buying the all-in-one job on special was a good idea. "Why not go for this Italian model over here which is half the size and twice the price?"

You know, it's the one which burns your hand every time you put something in it and has the little pictures on the control panel which are worn before you ever work out what they mean.

As for sinks, what do I know about recessing or bottle traps? Or ducting or venting? And why is it that the people who do know about those things often don't know about pulling their trousers up past their butt-cracks and employing a simple system we outsiders call a belt?

"So," the Ginger nervously enquired, "how are you getting on, then?"

"Actually," I answered. "I've gone off the idea of a kitchen and I think a lav will only clog up the plumbing."

What's wrong with dial-a-pizza and incontinence pants anyway?

Painting

IN A FIT OF SWEETNESS and loveliness, I told the Ginger I'd single-handedly paint our apartment. You know, the one which is still just an empty rectangle, owing to the pointyheads at the planning department still arguing over whether toilet has a "y" in it or not.

"Not having a bathroom or a kitchen or a bedroom or anything will make it all the easier," I enthused over what I can only assume now was one gin too many.

"Relax," I said. "Leave it to me. Piece of cake. No worries."

Why then, a week later, am I still coming up with long lists of very important things which I absolutely must get done before I can concentrate on the job at hand?

According to what I have written down so far, I must find world peace, lose it and find it again before I can so much as think about picking up a roller.

I must learn to sing and dance and play the piano, grow my hair, stop biting my nails, give up, um, everything twice, put my left foot in, put my left foot out, be abducted by aliens and have sex with Brad Pitt before so much as a drop of paint hits any one of those bare four walls.

In short why did I open my big, fat mouth?

Painting is for men with 10cm butt-crack or very young people whose bones don't already creak when they bend over to pick something up (these days, if it's worth less than $20 it can bloody well stay on the floor).

Sure, I've painted in the past. There was the black bedroom at home in the 1970s but it was small and I was still at school. There was a raft of Mexican red flats in the 1980s but there were helpers and they had casks of wine. There was room after room of Pearl Lustre in the 1990s but my powers over the Ginger were obviously stronger then, because all I had to do was come home and say, "Lovely. Oh, look, you missed a bit in the corner."

Now, he's coming home from work every day, asking me how

I'm getting on and if I've finished yet. I've taken to applying small blobs of toothpaste to my hair in a bid to look as though paint has sploshed on it, when the real truth is paint has not got anywhere near my person.

I got as far as the shop once but the people behind the counter were all swapping stories about friends who'd fallen off ladders on to their heads and it somehow put me off. Plus, I didn't really like the smell.

The thing is, the Ginger is coming to inspect the rectangle this weekend and I don't quite know how he's going to feel about the Gib-board type nature of the surroundings.

Especially as, in a fit of nervousness, I told him not only had I finished the job but I had applied a Michelangelo-style frieze to the ceiling in my spare time.

Obviously, the absence of such is going to prove something of a stumbling block but I've drawn up a list of my options at this stage.

One, actually paint it. Two, dye my hair and move to Hokitika. Three, wallpaper. Four, fire. Five, sprinklers. Six, locusts. Seven…

Living with Mum

WHEN I WAS LITTLE and used to dream about what I would be doing in the year 2000, living at home with Mum was strangely not on the list.

Mostly, I imagined I would be a famous vet, living in the Yorkshire countryside and writing books about sticking my hands up cows' bums.

However, since someone else got there first, the supermodel jobs were all taken, I never did manage to invent the pill which makes you thin and my acting career never went anywhere after playing Winnie the Pooh in 1976, here I am living at home with Mum.

Of course, this is only temporary. At least, that's what I have told her but the truth is I like it here.

The fridge is always full, the washing gets hung out, it's warm, the electric blanket magically gets turned on and there's often dinner on the table.

Someone does the housework, takes the rubbish out, picks up after you and makes cups of tea.

It's just like having a wife. In fact, I now see how the whole idea of wives caught on so well in the first place.

Could be we're in the honeymoon period of the whole moving home scenario but, with this in mind, I've already taken the precaution of hiding all the wooden spoons, should the situation take a turn for the worse.

I'm also trying very hard not to treat this house like a bloody hotel and am not going out looking like something out of the Corso bag. Nor am I smoking fags on the sly in the bathroom, secretly reading *79 Park Avenue* by Harold Robbins or nicking bottles of badly hidden gin from the garage. Actually, to be honest, I had a crack at the gin but it's obviously far better hidden these days.

The dog is very happy at Nana's, as there's an extra pair of adoring eyes to admire his handsome build and a spare set of hands to fondle his princely coat. The Ginger likes it for the same reason but without the fondling.

"Don't get too used to it here," he grumbled, though, as I sat in front of *Coro St* the other day, soaking my feet in the foot spa. "Don't forget there's a perfectly good, dark, small, empty rectangle with your name on it across town."

Oh, how I laughed. As if we'll ever live there! Why, I could train to be a builder, work for 25 years, retire, become an inspector and give myself the building consent before anybody else will do it. Really, Ginge, get a grip.

Imagine my surprise when he said it appeared the approval to build a kitchen and bathroom in our tiny apartment-to-be had, in fact, come through. I nearly choked on my box of Roses. The Out tray emptied, just like that? A miracle, no less.

So, let the butt-crack spotting commence!

Actually, I've been slightly disappointed by the calibre of the builders as they've reported for duty at the rectangle. Muscly and strapping the lot of them and not a centimetre of fleshy rear-end in sight.

Even more amazing, not a single radio playing talkback slightly off the station.

Actually, perhaps they're not real builders. Perhaps the rectangle will always be empty. Perhaps I'll have to stay at home with my mum till the year 3000. Oh, well.

Hard Yakka

NO MATTER HOW MANY men with thick fingers and extra bits hanging from their belts swore they were working around the clock, for weeks our empty rectangle remained an empty rectangle.

Finally, in a bid to actually turn our apartment into somewhere we might one day be able to live, I decided if you want a job done properly, you should do it yourself.

As it turns out, it's quite hard to decide what to wear when you are a tradesperson. And you thought those holey jumpers were just thrown on without a moment's thought, eh?

After a couple of days at the sewing machine, I came up with just the right combination of rip and splatter in a few sensible, breathable fabrics I knew could hold their own on any busy building site.

My first day on the job, I couldn't believe what a mess the rectangle had become.

All the men with extra bits hanging from their belts blamed all the other men with extra bits hanging from their belts.

Apparently, it's plasterers, electricians, plumbers and builders who leave the worst messes. Well, that only left me — and I was the one cleaning up.

All the leftover bits of wood and pipe and wire and plastic I had to pile into large plastic bags and store in the garage. The nails and screws had to be picked up and biffed. The floor had to be swept and swept and swept again until only one layer of crunchy stuff to walk on remained.

It took a day. I went home exhausted.

The next day was spent mostly answering questions. "Where's my leftover bit of wood/pipe/wire/plastic?" was pretty much the gist of it, with a few "What happened to my nails/screws?" thrown in and a fine sprinkling of more crunchy stuff to finish.

The next couple of days I spent painting while the plasterer plastered. He was under the mistaken impression I was called

"Bro" but I didn't mind too much, because he'd had the good grace to turn up only five days late.

By now, my hands looked worthy of a belt with extra bits hanging from it, sticking plasters hopefully included. Nearly every finger sported an inexplicable cut, complete with a smear of fresh blood, I had three callouses and a blood blister which still makes it hard to type the letters O and I.

I spent the following day lining the gib board in the rectangle's tiny bathroom while the tiler tiled. Oh, the things we talked about! I was quite tired by the end of the day, especially around the ears, but there was still one more top corner to go.

Dragging the ladder into the bathroom closet, I climbed to the top and lifted my brush to start. Suddenly, I felt a breeze swirling around my lower back. I froze. Slowly, I let the brush drop to the floor and, hardly daring to breathe, descended the ladder. Finding the soon-to-be-hung mirror propped up against the wall, I stood with my back to it, craned my neck and revealed my worst nightmare.

I had butt-crack.

Without any encouragement from me, my jeans had mysteriously crept down to the unacceptable level displayed on building sites all around the country.

That was it. My helping days were over.

The Festive Season

That Time of Year

AROUND THIS TIME OF YEAR, I am comforted to know I am not the only one in a stage of almost permanent crankiness — it's almost epidemic.

A quick ring around of my friends has revealed not one single husband and wife couple are talking to each other — for reasons varying from arguments over the TV remote to the sheer stupid pig ignorance of the male species.

And most children, by the same token, seem extremely lucky not to be locked in a dark cupboard with nothing to eat but stale bread and pond scum until New Year 2015.

One harried mum I know told me she had fallen victim to a combination of the Harry Potter hype and a chain store discount and bought, at the constant, nagging behest of her small son, all four of the boy wizard books.

No sooner had she handed the popular tomes over, however, than the ungrateful child — with barely so much as a glance — demanded he be taken immediately to the $2 shop where there is apparently lots of "cool stuff".

If he were mine, I'd have called the taxidermist.

But then, I have abandoned my usual flawlessly sweet and even temper in favour of a state of almost permanent irritation which has had the Ginger spending most the past week hiding in his shed — a fact I find all the more annoying because he doesn't even have a shed.

"Is it something I've done?" he asked sweetly from behind the sofa yesterday, holding the garbage bin lid over his head to avoid missiles.

"Did you make the hair on my legs grow infeasibly fast, my swimming togs shrink, my bank balance overdrawn?" I growled. "Is it your fault I haven't given the slightest thought to Christmas shopping but bought a pair of sandals for myself that pinch my two little toes and give me blisters on the bottom of my foot?

"Can I blame you for the war on terrorism and the starving

millions and floods and droughts and volcano eruptions and Jennifer Aniston getting to Brad Pitt before I did? Well, can I?"

There was a small silence.

"I'm not quite sure," he finally offered, "but I think the answer is probably yes."

I had forgotten we go through this every year — the pre-Christmas-stress blues. They start the moment you realise that, just as you have finally got used to writing one year in your chequebook, it's time for the next one.

They progress when you overhear a pretty, blonde, thin woman in front of you at the supermarket telling the check-out girl she finished her Christmas shopping in July and is going home to fashion an angel for the top of the tree out of old Rolex watches given her by adoring ex-boyfriends.

They proceed when you take your body out of hiding and reveal it at the beach, only to have small children run away screaming while big clumps of emotional lads yell at you to get your gear ON.

"'Tis the season to be jolly," the Ginger reminded me.

"'Tis actually the bit before the season to be jolly," I corrected him, "which is otherwise known as the season to be hopelessly disorganised and on the brink of a nervous breakdown."

There was another small silence. "Perhaps we could move that season forward a bit," he suggested. "Or even combine it with the mid-winter, post-birthday season to be another bloody year older and still crap at everything. What do you think?"

I think it's a good thing I married Pollyanna, not Scrooge.

Drinks

AS A PERSON who's been written up in international medical textbooks for not containing so much as a single shred of willpower, I find the Christmas drinks circuit particularly hard going.

But you won't find me on the office photocopier with a pair of novelty knickers or anything — it's just I'm physically incapable of saying no to a snifter or two.

And while in my wild and crazy youth I could knock back a string of margaritas and get up and go for a run at 5am the following morning, now, a mere three glasses of wine has me waking up 10 hours later to a symphony of nasty little men banging at the inside of my head with pick axes.

This doesn't put me off the Yuletide festivities, you understand. No, I just accept that, around this time of year, I'll spend an unfeasibly large amount of time reading very fat books about changing my religion to one which doesn't let you drink any alcohol — i.e. the opposite of Catholicism.

I combine this with an hourly ritual of thanking God that the liver is worn inside the body, rather than exposed in a public fashion — say, on one's forehead.

Now that the drinking age has been lowered to 18, though, I would like to save the younger generation from the follies of overtippling by passing on some of my hard-won knowledge.

My first bit of advice is, don't drink.

In my experience, drinking only causes smoking of fags, which costs you a fortune and kills you, or drunkenness, which costs you a fortune and makes you look like someone who doesn't know how to put their lipstick on properly.

My second bit of advice is, if you are going to drink, stop soon after you have started.

This will save you from any embarrassment, such as getting home from the work Christmas party with streamers on the inside of your tights and no idea how they got there, as happened to a friend of mine some years ago.

My young neighbour recently regaled me with a similar tale of a friend of hers, who went to a Halloween party dressed as a witch and woke up next morning minus her wand, hat, cloak and fake nose (with warts) but plus a large pumpkin.

The neighbour herself had accidentally overtippled at a party the previous weekend and had not only had the good sense to call a taxi to come and get her as soon as she felt queasy but had asked the driver to stop at a gas station halfway home, so she could borrow a bucket. And they say the young are silly! My third bit of advice is, if you are going to drink and not stop soon after you have started, get someone to follow your progress with a video camera or tape recorder.

Play it back the next day after your breakfast fry-up and you'll be amazed at how all your hilarious witticisms and high-spirited hi-jinks of the fun-filled night before seem nowhere near as humourous in the cold, hard light of day.

You really thought you were the first person to put an actual lampshade on your head?

You see, it's all about momentum. I'm sorry, I meant menstruation. Did I say moratorium? No, no, that should be millennium.

MODERATION. That's it, That's the key. Whew! I thought I'd forgotten it there for a moment.

Christmas

NEVER MIND decking the halls with boughs of holly and good will to all men — yeah, right.

Real-life Christmas is more traditionally a time of pulling out hair, screaming at kids and travelling to places you never even wanted to pass through, let alone stop in, so you can eat dried-up old buzzard with in-laws who can't remember your name (thanks to the fact you can still get sherry in flagons).

So don't worry if you spend all Boxing Day hiding in the boot of the car with a two-tier box of chocolates, crying.

You are not on your own. In fact, you're probably in the majority.

You see, before Christmas was about buying those ungrateful leeches you call children the right brand of high-tops, it was actually a religious festival celebrating the birth of... Oh, you know — there was a stable and three wise men came bearing booty.

One brought frankincense (which has since been outlawed because it smells like marijuana), another brought myrrh (which, being fake armpit hair, never really took off in the present-giving department) and the third man brought gold. So, really, there was one wise man and two dunderheads. Now, there's a surprise.

Somewhere along the line, that 2000-year-old tradition of giving gold to each other at Christmas got translated into socks and underpants (if you're the father), a nightie (if you're the mother) and a range of plastic goods designed to last approximately 21 hours (if you are a kid).

Also, nowhere in ancient records does it mention the wise man having to get immediately back on his camel and travel overnight to his sister-in-law's house — even though his mother's place is so much more central and she isn't a vegetarian.

Neither does it record the wise man's nieces and nephews spitting into the ground and screaming, "Gold? You gave us gold, again? Doh! We wanted platinum, you $%&*@!"

Can't you just see the poor dolt sitting under his camel with a sackful of candied dates, sobbing, "I AM wise, I AM wise"?

I've combed the Good Book for a decent ham recipe — nothing — and, as far as I can tell, there are no references in either the Old or New Testaments to shopping till your fingers bleed from fumbling for your credit cards.

It's time we got back to basics, I reckon.

For a start, let's make it all about mums. I'm sure that was the idea in the first place. Also, it's a good way of making sure no one else in the family works up any enthusiasm about participating. All shopping must be done by everybody else but Mum for Mum — and there'll be no rushing out to the 24-hour gas station at the last minute, either, thank you.

Presents must consist only of gold — although diamonds will do.

There will be no contact with in-laws over this downsized festive period and nothing bigger than the head of the youngest member of the family will be put in the oven or stuffed.

The kids will make Mum breakfast in bed, go to church and play quietly among themselves for the day, while all dads will go to the shed and practise being wise for a bit.

Now, that would be worth a fa-la-la-la-la or two, wouldn't it?

The Christmas After

IF I HEAR ONE more person say they hate Christmas, I will poke out their eyes with peppermint walking sticks. It's a time of peace and love and joy for crissakes!

Isn't the fact every meal from now until next year will have ham in it reason enough to give praise? No? Try these then:

1. Nibbles

You really MUST celebrate a time of year when you don't have to worry about the fat content of a peanut, because the baby Jesus said so. It's in the Bible.

The festive period is rife with salty snack foods and it is downright agnostic not to get among them. Also, all food eaten during religious festivals has no calories by order of special dispensation from the Pope herself.

2. Tipples

It is impossible to get bogged down by the fact our dollar is worth less than half a Guatemalan yak turd when there are so many free drinks to be had.

Once a year, at the work Christmas party, you are allowed to over tipple in front of your workmates and snog your boss in the photocopying room, so you really should make the most of it.

When you wake up aching from the pain of the stolen stationery stashed inside your brassiere and retching at the sudden memory of "Acne" George from accounts doing disgusting things with the staple gun, you will be grateful for your own husband and kids. You will never be able to look at a bottle of Malibu again. These are good things.

3. Shopping

So what if you have to sell Grandma to put enough petrol in the car to drive to the Freezer Failure Turkey Sale at the local mall? Why, that's just one less person to spend your yak turds on and she probably has enough past its use-by date bubble bath by now anyway.

As there is only one day a year when you get presents without having to pay the price of turning a year older, you should treat others as you wish to be treated yourself.

I'm just at the end of my year-long campaign to make sure the Ginger never again as long as he lives considers a Swiss Army pocketknife WITHOUT a corkscrew an acceptable token of his deep and abiding love for me.

"Anything which doesn't come in a tiny velvet box will be planted where the sun don't shine. Anything which doesn't come in a tiny velvet box will be planted where the sun don't shine." These were the words which finally got him released from a month-long confinement in the kitchen cupboard.

4. Wrapping

Keep in mind the person hired to do the free gift-wrapping at the store is quite possibly the boss's niece and therefore may be handicapped in the ribbon and bow department. Experts say you can put your post-Christmas nervous breakdown off by at least three hours by wrapping your presents yourself, even if you do have to tear the wallpaper off the sitting room walls and make ribbons from your undies to do it.

5. Holidays

In light of what happened at the office Christmas party, spending a week locked in a one-room motel with a batch of screaming kids and a belching husband seems pretty enticing. If in doubt, think ham and peanuts.

6. Chocolate

Refer to aforementioned Papal blessing.

Merry Christmas.

New Year

THERE'S ONLY GOING to be a select handful of resolutions this year but they're all biggies.

For a start, I hereby resolve never, ever, as long as I live, as long as there's life in these bones and breath in these lungs, not for all the tea in China — or India, where it mostly comes from these days — am I ever, ever, EVER going to move again. Ever.

Should you get wind of me even so much as thinking about packing things in a box, please track me down and give me a good slapping.

It's not the going places which makes me break out in boils. It's the getting my worldly goods there with me, in one piece, on the right day, without all the things you sleep on being missing in action, no sign of the dog kennel and huge dents in the fridge.

I will try to remember the phrase "Sweet as a nut, mate" is a good thing, despite my experience to the contrary, and I pledge to curb my urge to leave burning paper bags full of dog poop at the offices of a certain countrywide moving company.

Secondly, I resolve to cut down on my grudge-bearing and don't think that lets you off the hook, you bad-moving b******s. I'm cutting down, not giving up.

However, I hereby pledge the really bitter and twisted dog-poop part of my grudges will now have a statute of limitations of just two years and all grudges will be dropped after a period of 10 years.

This lets the humiliating PE teacher, the first boyfriend and the boss with the small-man complex off the hook but still leaves me plenty to be getting on with.

I also resolve to try to not be such a pain-in-the-butt reformed smoker.

It's now five months since the last gasper passed these lips and, to my own horror and amazement, I have turned into the sort of person whose nostrils I used to dream about abusing with giant matchsticks. I wave my hand in front of my face when a puff of smoke goes by, grimace in an ugly fashion if a passer-by lights up and hang my clothes outside, disgusted, after five seconds in the very same smoky bars from whence only a fire alarm could previously have removed me.

This year, I am going to try to re-integrate with the smokers even if it kills me, which we all know it very well could.

Finally, I am going to cease and desist moaning about my job or lack thereof. This may have something to do with the fact the Ginger, after many months of me whingeing in his ear about not having anyone to talk to, has found work for my semi-idle hands. With him. As his assistant. On a film.

"What if I get tired?" I asked in a frightened voice when he presented me with my new career.

"You'd have to do something pretty bad for me to fire you," he answered solemnly.

"TIRED not FIRED!" I shrieked. He would fire me? Not if I quit first. Or sued, you know, for harassment.

Perhaps, while I'm here, I should resolve not to instigate litigation against the poor Ginger when he's really such a nice chap.

A new year? Sweet as a nut, mate.

And I mean it.

Another New Year

I'VE JUST LOOKED back at the column I wrote on the first of January and it is with some horror that I realise I've kept all my New Year's resolutions. What a loser. What a grown-up, responsible, unimaginative, do-good loser.

There's absolutely no point in making resolutions if you are going to keep them — everybody knows that. Only the very old, the infirm and the extremely boring keep their New Year's resolutions.

The rest of us spend five minutes on New Year's Eve contemplating how badly we've failed, then hoe into the Baileys Irish Cream with tequila chasers like normal people.

How did I get here so quickly, then? I'm not even 40 — and I can still name the Prime Minister.

I promised a year ago that I would never move house again and now, a year later, I haven't so much as looked at a single cardboard box — let alone filled it with junk I didn't want in the first place and will want even less when it gets somewhere new.

I resolved to cut down on my grudge-bearing, giving feelings of extreme bitterness and twistedness a statute of limitations of just two years.

This I have done and I've proved it — in one case letting an old cow I should rightfully poke in the eyes gush all over me and even give me a friendly squeeze. I pledged I would try to not be such a pain-in-the-butt reformed smoker. This I have also managed. For one whole year, not so much as a tip of a gasper passed my lips and I revelled in waving my hands in front of my face and pooh-poohing all those poor wretches still addicted.

But once the year passed, I released my grip. Didn't notice other people's butt-headedness and even slipped and had a couple of fags myself, late at night and under the influence of chardonnay.

Finally, I vowed I was going to cease and desist moaning about my job, or lack thereof.

And what do you know, I finally managed to work out how to make a living from writing books, which I love, therefore leaving me with nothing to moan about.

Obviously, I set my sights too mind-numbingly low.

Well, I'm not making the same mistake this year, I can tell you.

This year, I resolve to get down to a size 10 and wear nothing but midriff-revealing clothes for at least three months of the year. I resolve to not lie in bed pretending to be asleep until the Ginger delivers my crumpets. I resolve to let my leg hair grow and embrace my inner Sasquatch.

I am going to do all my Christmas shopping by Valentine's Day, remember birthdays of people I don't even know, put all of my photos — even the ones with no people in them — in albums and vacuum under the bed every single time.

This year, I really am going to give up meat, even bacon. Even lamb shanks. Even eye fillet. I'm going to have only one cup of coffee a day and always drink eight glasses of water.

I am going to stop pretending I bought full-fat milk by accident and buy it on purpose. I am going to enjoy exercising instead of treating it like a punishment and I am going to play a team sport, just for fun.

This year, I am going to climb Mount Everest, record my own CD, go to the black hole of Calcutta and work with the underprivileged and fly to the moon.

There — that's more like it. I feel better now.